Stage Fright:
Who Needs It?

Gordon Goodman, Ph.D.

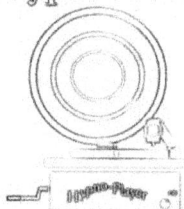

Illustrations by Gordon Goodman.
ISBN: 978-0615925271
NuWerks Publishing, USA
Under the division of *HypnoCast* Educational Products

Stage Fright: Who Needs it?

DEDICATION

To my parents.

CONTENTS

Dr. Gordon Goodman

ACKNOWLEDGMENTS

Dr. Paul Salamunovich. Seth Riggs. Robert Hunter. Chris Bearde. Dr. Bernard Luskin. Jerry Herman. Glenn Casale. Giorgio Tozzi. James Whitmore, Jr.. Craig T. Nelson. Barry Levinson. Scott Henderson. Dr. James Kaufman. Dr. Jean Pierre Isbouts. Bruce Colell. S.L. Goodman. Gwyn Goodman. And my wife Alison.

Dr. Gordon Goodman

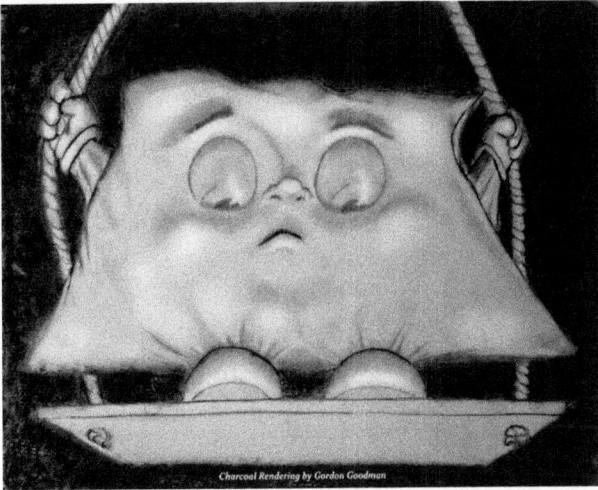

Charcoal Rendering by Gordon Goodman

1. DEFINITION: WHAT IS STAGE FRIGHT?

Imagine you, right now, dressed up in a tight gold leotard walking a tightrope two hundred feet in the air with no net. Imagine sitting in a cage filled with hungry lions. Imagine having a ticking bomb strapped to your back while a poisonous snake is crawling up your leg. Imagine knowing these things are going to happen tomorrow, and that you have no way of stopping them.

That's what it's like to have stage fright.

We've searched for a cure to stage fright, performance anxiety, evaluation apprehension...whatever you want to call it, for years and years, and still, even in the 21st century, the fear of performing before an audience is one of the most common forms of anxiety humans encounter. It affects athletes, artists, public speakers, politicians, even electronic gamers. It affects muscle movement and decision-making. It can change how we think about ourselves and how we're thought of by others. In other words, it can be a real pain in the ass.

Maybe that's not the way you'd expect a psychologist to talk, but I think it's about time we put stage fright in its place. It's an obstruction to human performance. It's unnecessary. And if you suffer from it, it's about time you knew the truth.

Stage fright is completely avoidable.

Stage fright occurs because:

1. You are unprepared for the task you are about to perform.
2. Because the performance is extremely important to your future, social standing, and/or your self-worth.
3. Because past performance experiences have conditioned you into having anxiety before you perform.
4. Because there are distractions that interfere with concentration and attention.
5. More commonly: It's a combination of all these conditions.

We'll talk a lot about stage fright, take it apart and look at the pieces. I want to make you an expert on performance anxiety so that you can approach it like a mechanic rather than someone who's caught in a tornado. Stage fright is an emotional and biological reaction. Often there is no logical reason at all to have it. But it can be avoided. It can be disassembled. You can pour anti-freeze into your engine.

I want to warn the reader that I repeat myself a lot. I *believe* in repetition because it helps form long-term memory. You may be irritated with me for this. There is no recourse for this except to burn the book after you memorize it. I really don't care as long as what I'm saying gets into that thick skull of yours.

My goal is to make you bulletproof. I'm not going to coddle you or try to bolster your self-esteem. We've learned that self-esteem can't be gained by talking. I'm here to make you into a stainless steel performer, one who trains effectively, and one who can count on their training and ability in any situation. A successful performance doesn't occur by chance, or when all the conditions are right. A successful performance can occur even when situations are crazy and unpredictable. A successful performance is something you can count on and repeat over and over, with confidence and absolute control. Stage fright isn't abnormal. It happens to the greatest performers in the world. It's part of our standard equipment. It's a cognitive loop that *only* occurs if other people are watching. It does not occur when you are absolutely alone.

Stage fright, or performance anxiety (for you athletes), communication anxiety (for you public speakers) is a form of stress. Worrying about an upcoming performance can start months before the event and precede any physical symptoms of stress, or it can be triggered by signs of stress given off by the body just prior to the event. We have anxiolytic drugs that work on the brain to decrease anxiety. We have beta-blockers that control how our body deals with adrenaline. These drugs artificially control emotional responses such as fear and panic, and our physical responses such as a pounding heart and shaking hands.

Adrenaline, part of our flight or fight system, can

be a plus or minus. It can help when we need strength and speed, but it gets in the way when we need fine motor control and concentration. Adrenaline isn't bad. Not at all. Most performers perform with some excess of adrenaline. It's our imagination that makes adrenaline the bad guy. Stage fright occurs because we humans have the ability to imagine. Humans, unlike other animals, can use our imagination to turn on our evolutionary survival mechanisms. Once these mechanisms are turned on, they can't be turned off until the threat disappears, and in the case of stage fright, that means removing the audience or any possible judgment from others. Performers generally can't say to an audience "Please leave." So we're stuck with 'em. Sometimes we try to anticipate what the audience is thinking about us...but that overuse of our imaginative processes eats up mental processing space until we no longer have any power left for our performance. It distracts us so much we can forget what we're doing. We're wired that way. All animals are wired that way.

We're built to behave differently when other humans are around.

Actually, having others around can help our performance. It depends how complicated the task and how important it is. Simple tasks do better under stress, complicated ones fare worse. The thing is, other animals don't have this ability to imagine. They just react because of things going on in the real world. But humans, we have this kinky ability to use our imagination to predict future outcomes. We had it when we were facing woolly mammoths and saber-toothed tigers without a spear. We could imagine ourselves being tromped on or munched. We ran to a cave because we pictured it in our imagination as a way to escape. We're still on this planet because our imagination helped us anticipate and avoid danger.

In our present age, we often imagine dangers that don't exist. Now we imagine ourselves being trampled on and munched by other people's judgment. Our brain triggers the same systems in the brain that the woolly mammoth once did. I don't know whom that insults the most, humans, or the mammoth.

Don't get me wrong. It's great to have an imagination. Every great accomplishment of mankind was the result of this ability. But when we have to perform in front of an audience, imagining the future simply gets in the way. It doesn't help us to avoid danger; it becomes a danger in itself. So what's the answer?

Most self-help books are written by modern-day snake oil salesmen. You can say anything and claim it helps people. Anything. After all, one third of all patients got better after bloodletting. Plus a lot of self-help jargon comes from the obvious. It's called the Barnum Effect. Fortune tellers rely on it. And yes, some individuals need to be told not to put their finger in the light socket. And others want to believe that some guru possesses wisdom greater than their own.

Well...your magic is just as good as anyone else's.

Anybody with a big enough ego can write a book, which is quite a statement considering the amount of books in the world. These books can make fantastic promises that sound great and make people feel good for a while. They offer new beliefs that can prompt new behaviors. These beliefs can act as placebos, and we know that a good percentage of patients improve simply by believing they are going to. So you witch doctors out there...you still have career opportunities.

A lot of self-help authors regurgitate old ideas, give them new names, and pass them off as their own. This helps authors sell workshops. Self-help will always exist because what they're REALLY selling is *hope*, not cures. Hope is a key component of our lives. When hope is missing, or blocked from view, humans take a nose-dive into a lake of depression.

It's important to know that stage fright doesn't go away by patting someone on the back and telling them not to be scared. Stage fright has been around since we first started hunting, and drawing on cave walls, and having sex. The moment we were able to become a critic, stage fright was born. We know a lot about stage fright...yet we still can't predict it. Humans differ, situations differ and as long as that's true, stage fright will always be an unpredictable animal.

Our evolutionary survival mechanisms and our imaginations are to blame for stage fright. Although we can't live without these things, they have the ability to set off false alarms in our body and mind whenever we're being watched. It's pretty hard to turn the alarms off once they start.

Most people react to stage fright by trying to fight it. This doesn't work too well. The real trick is to find some process that bypasses the alarms in the first place. I'll be talking about the ways to accomplish this. A big part of it comes from preparation, but nobody wants to hear that because it's a lot of work and it's boring. Training processes take time and effort and today we're conditioned to have instant results. But if you want to be able to walk into any situation and perform with confidence, you're best bet is to train well and train scientifically.

Most of the performers you watch and admire are not wunderkinds. Even Mozart, Andre Agassi, Michael Jackson, or Tom Hanks. They are people who have fears and insecurities just like you, but who have put in thousands of hours training. But simple repetition is not enough. You need to train smart.

Performing is simple. Monkeys can do it. You train. You perform. You take your award, your money, your applause, your self-satisfaction, pack up your skis, your track shoes, your briefcase, your dance shoes, your make-up...and go home. That's it. It's a job. It can be a wonderful job. But it's a job. It's a task and to be good at a task you need to practice. That's why stage fright can be confusing. Our imagination tends to shine the spotlight on our *fear of the audience* instead of the job.

REAL danger, shuts down all other processes except the ones that help you fight or flee. So our focus on the job or the task gets stolen and handed over to our fear. IMAGINING danger does the exact same thing. Stage fright only happens when we imagine that we'll screw up and because of that screw up, something bad will happen. Right? So stage fright focuses on failure – stealing from our ability NOT to fail.

Well...that's just crazy.

I wrote this book to help you get back to what

you're supposed to be doing. The body of this book will help you understand the mental and physiological components of stage fright. This will help you understand how you are a biological machine.

IF YOU HAVE A PUBLIC PERFORMANCE SOON, SKIP TO SECTION TWO NOW.

Your process will be different than everyone else's because your genetics, your history, and the type of task you're performing is different. Although the steps of the overall process are generic, the length of each step will depend on you. The object of this book is to teach you how to pass through an alternate corridor, one that won't trigger evolutionary mechanisms, or generate imaginary threats.

Performers belong to an exclusive club.

Have you ever looked at jugglers or sketch artists and thought, "Man, I wish I could do that", as if it were some inborn talent? We seldom think about the hundreds, maybe thousands of hours those people practice. Human performance is mostly a matter of time, effort, and some talent. All animals can be conditioned to perform a targeted behavior. When you pay your dues as a performer, putting in those lonely hours of practice, those early performances that help you to hone and craft your task, you earn a membership card to a very exclusive club. The Performer's Club.

Those in the Performer's Club:

    1. All rehearse and train.

2. All learn at different speeds.

3. All have moments when they worry about failing.

4. Each stage of learning has it's own identity.

Early stages are filled with: "Oh my God! This is
hopeless! I'll never be able to do this." Middle stages
are filled with: "Oh my God why can't I *get* this! I
know what to do and I'm not doing it...what's wrong
with my brain!" Ending stages are filled with: "Oh my
God! I can't do this anymore! Everybody else has a
life and here I am working night and day on this crap!
I'm done! I'm bored! I'm going crazy!"

Smart professionals try to avoid mind chatter by
handing the responsibility of over to the training process itself. That's why athletes have coaches. Athletes
hand the responsibility of learning and improving their
skill over to the coach. Coaches place the athlete into a
training process that has worked successfully in the
past. If you work alone instead of with a coach, you
still have to hand the responsibility over your training
process and over to time. Even if you know it works,
it's *still going to take time*. Time is very important.
We require repetition and time to learn things long-
term. When you establish your training stages, you also
have to allow for time periods that are required by each
stage.

Everybody... with very few exceptions... (and you
might not want to meet those exceptions in a dark alley)
has doubts about their ability to impress or satisfy a
crowd, an expert, a coach, opposing team members,
fellow team members, or themselves – it doesn't matter
if you're a famous actor, politician, evangelist, athlete,

9

or musician. Evaluation by others is a bitch. Professionals develop training processes that will make what they do automatic. That way even if you *do* worry about evaluation, your body will just keep going, doing the right things automatically. Pros rely on automatic processes. If you're *not* a pro, you don't have as much proof, but that's okay. You will, trust me.

Sure, you'll run into savants who innately are able to do a task without preparation. These people are few and far between and many of them don't pursue their gifts because it's not challenging enough for them. Most of the people you *think* are savants have spent countless hours preparing just to give you that impression.

Design your training process to automate your task. That's the whole purpose of training. Practice until you can perform the task without thinking. By automating your task you can concentrate on the *way* you perform your task, instead of *how* you perform the task. The mechanical aspects of a task are boring. It's how you shape your performance that turns it into art and makes it exciting.

So strap yourself in and start. Don't think about when the training will end, just start - and keep the schedule you set. Like a Black Ops soldier, your training process should become your religion. You will learn to have faith in it as long as you're honest and keep the schedules you set. Okay...here we go...

2. EVOLUTIONARY BEHAVIOR: THE ORIGINS OF THREAT

We've all seen herd behavior, but you may not know *why* herds form. Very simply, animals form herds because it's a way of disappearing. Deep inside a herd, the spotlight disappears and predators have a hard time picking you out from the crowd. However, if you're hanging around on the outside of the herd, by yourself, you're an easy target because you're now an individual. Any *thing*, or any *one*, who sticks out as an individual, is going to get attention. In certain situations you get awards, power, and money; in other situations you become lunch.

Inside a herd you're part of a mob. You lose individuality and essentially disappear. Evolutionary theory proposes that losing your individuality can increase your chances of remaining in the gene pool, and most of us don't want to get out of that pool. In fact, being anonymous is so safe it tends to set humans free to act in socially unacceptable ways. Mobs commit criminal acts with abandon because, as part of a mob, individuals feel invisible. You can't be punished if you're invisible, but neither can you be a star.

So, the more separate an object is from the norm, the more noticeable it becomes. In statistics these objects are called "outliers". Being an outlier can have its advantages. While sticking out around predators can get you killed, sticking out around the opposite sex increases the possibilities of getting lucky.

Most humans want to be special. People work hard to look and act uniquely. We develop special ways of walking, standing, talking, dressing, or grooming. Humans have this quirky need to know we exist, and getting noticed is the fastest way of satisfying that need. Sticking out gives us a unique identity and also gives us a reason to create. The things we create extend our identity beyond our own physical bodies, and carry our unique identity, our brand, on through time and space, increasing our value. People with low self-esteem tend to create less. People who have extremely high, perhaps overbearing self-esteem, create more, because their self-importance eliminates doubt. Their work isn't better than yours, mind you. They just create more of it.

Putting our identity under a spotlight, begs for public judgment. Just as failure can decrease our social economic value, success can increase it. *Celebrity = Power* in most cases. Even if that celebrity comes from an immoral or socially inappropriate act. The fact is: Humans have pretty short moral memories. While infamy can mean an immediate fall from grace, in the long term, most people only remember the fame part, not the infamy part. Failure is more temporary than we think. Mere exposure, just getting your name or face in front of people, is a "win" any way you look at it. It increases your social value and likability (yes that's a real word). You can be a famous president, or a famous prostitute, and over time, fame and infamy lose their polarity. You become simply: famous.

Just like the animals on the outside of the herd, people in the spotlight gain the attention of fans and predators. Celebrity attracts threats, kidnapping, and slander. Celebrity by proxy can make a person or product famous by being *associated* with someone famous. Fame rubs off. Greatness by association is alive and well. Men and women throughout the ages have slept their way to greatness, leveling the playing field. Having sex with a famous person is one of the fastest ways to feel like an equal. You become a celebrity if you sleep with a celebrity. At least for a day or two. It also explains why so many people in the public eye need protection. Many people are attracted to fame, and trying to get a piece of that pie any way they can, even by murder.

So, is standing out from the herd worth it?

Evolutionary biologists would say "yes". Sexual partners are certainly more available to those in the spotlight. Financial rewards are also usually greater for those who stand out from the herd. A celebrity can make money simply by associating their face or name with a commercial product. For example, according to Forbes Magazine, Michael Phelps, the Olympic gold medalist, currently gained a net worth of $40 million dollars by adding his name or picture to commercial products. So fame can be lucrative. The problem is, fame isn't something we can really predict.

According to Dr. James Kaufman, an expert on creativity, stardom can occur because of talent, practice, location in time and space, or all of these factors. What exactly causes the jump from a working professional to superstardom is impossible to predict. We just don't know why it happens. And the percentage of performers who do make it to superstardom is small.

The higher your fame rises, the further you have to fall. This risk of falling is a subconscious threat waiting in the shadows, haunting some performers throughout their career. Jerry Seinfeld had a fear that his career would plummet long after he reached stardom. For some performers, falling from grace is a constant threat, like the blade of a guillotine hanging over their neck. This is a problem. While short periods of threat or risk are associated with excitement and challenge, long periods of threat or risk can be physically and mentally damaging. Like a clutch on a car (although clutches on cars are rare anymore), risk engages your body's autonomic survival mechanisms.

For a performer, risk occurs when identity is attached to the task. Your brand is at stake, your name, and your reputation, not to mention your financial livelihood. Things get a lot more stressful when your identity is threatened. While a moderate amount of risk can be exhilarating, an overwhelming amount of risk over a long period of time can cause cognitive impairment and even affect memory-making processes in the hippocampus.

Basically, when stress levels are too high, our frontal cortex gets all discombobulated (the scientific term) because cognitive functions start shutting down to allow for fight or flight, strength and speed. Emotion becomes a bully and pushes reasonable thought out a sixth story window.

IMPORTANT: When we perform in front of an audience, we always interpret the situation based on its *threat potential*.

The major threats triggering stage fright are:

1. The difficulty of the task.

2. Its importance to monetary gain and future employment.

3. Its importance to the performer's public and self-image.

3. The importance of the people in the audience.

Moderate threat can be good for a performance, as long as the task isn't too hard and doesn't require a lot of cognitive control. Too little threat means your arousal mechanisms may not even bother to kick in and help. This leads to poorer performance and boredom. Too much threat means your arousal may end up choking you out on the mat. Generally speaking, we know that a little threat makes the game more interesting.

We all have genetically inherited activity levels of arousal, so we all react to threat differently to stress. I've provided a short test later on to help you categorize yourself as an introvert or extravert. If you score very high, you're an introvert. If you score low, you're an extravert. It's simplistic, but it works well enough.

Just like animals in the wild, some individuals are incredibly aware of possible dangers and are hyper-vigilant (introverts). Others don't dwell on the dangers, but are driven by the rewards of performing (extra-verts). You can lean either way and still be a great per-former. If you're an introvert, you'll probably require more preparation to feel safe. Try to eliminate sur-prises. If you're an extravert you may relish surprises and have to watch that you don't get so bored that you cut short your training process.

3. WHEN THE BODY HAS A MIND OF ITS OWN

As I mentioned before, early in the 20th century a number of biologists studied the effects of stress on performance in animals. To induce stress, researchers used electric shocks, or would flood the cages with water so they could watch their behavior under pressure. For some reason we're not allowed to run these tests on humans. I'm sure there are people you'd *like* to test this way, but remember: Humans don't need actual physical threat to experience stress. They can get stressed just by *imagining* a stressful situation. Thoughts, in the form of worry can cause physiological changes that are no different than those experienced during physical threat.

Interestingly, physiological arousal in "challenge" conditions (excitement) seems to be the same as those in "threat" conditions (fear), except possibly for a difference in vascular constriction. Vascular constriction is greater in conditions of threat and help our fight or flight system. The neurotransmitters GABA, serotonin, dopamine, and norepinephrine are all major players too.

In non-primates, the limbic system would be the source of most stress, but with primates you never can tell. We have that pesky frontal cortex that has its tendrils wrapped insidiously around the limbic system so it's hard to tell how much fear is real or imagined. Once anxiety exists, a signal is sent to the hypothalamus, which sends an alert out to the body - adrenaline speeds up the heart, creating deeper pulmonary contractions, cortisol begins to shut down functions that are not immediately necessary, shifting us into hyper-vigilance.

This sounds like a major process, but physiological arousal happens all the time without our conscious awareness. You can think of arousal as having two-stages.

1. The physiological symptoms

2. The label we give those physiological symptoms.

We first notice our own physiological arousal - then look around, looking for clues as to *why* we're aroused. If the situation seems fearful, we'll label the emotion fear; if it seems like we're enjoying ourselves, we'll label the arousal *excitement*. This process happens below the conscious level. By the time we wake up to it, we've already labeled the emotion.

Arousal is generic.

Donald Dutton and Arthur Aron conducted an experiment where males were sent across two bridges.

One bridge was a scary rope bridge; the other bridge was a non-scary bridge. An attractive female was sent across the bridge while each male crossed his respective bridge. Those crossing the scary bridge had greater sexual arousal than those crossing the safe bridge. These led the researchers to conclude that fear from the scary bridge was being interpreted as another kind of arousal, sexual arousal. They concluded that we get aroused first, then look for a reason for that arousal. The males crossing the scary bridge sought to ask the female out on a date more than those males crossing the boring bridge. They interpreted the arousal caused by the bridge, as being caused by the female.

The interesting thing about physiological arousal is that, by itself, it's harmless. It's only when arousal is labeled as something bad, that gives us problems. In small amounts, arousal can be fun and makes the activity challenging. Any time you challenge yourself to do better, you risk something. You don't risk much, but enough to make the activity engaging. That's why people play video games. A tiny bit of risk increases the excitement and satisfaction of winning. Because of risk, winning, even getting the right answer in class, releases neurotransmitters associated with pleasure.

Performance Task + Small Amount of Risk = Challenge (fun)
Performance Task + Huge Amount of Risk = Threat (no fun)

When there's too much at risk, the challenge of the situation drains away along with the fun. Clouds roll in, and things get threatening. Lightning shoots in and out of our brain, causing the autonomic nervous system to arouse the body.

With our ability to imagine, we can start worrying about an upcoming threat months before it happens. Once threat exceeds our confidence, we start the stage fright spiral. That's when conditioned behavior, auto-mation of the task, becomes so important. When we're so distracted that we can't think, those hours of practice to make our task automatic are well worth it. It keeps us going without thinking.

Even with high levels of confidence, threat can grow and reach a tipping point, dropping us into an ocean of fear. If threat levels are low or moderate, or if confidence levels are high, the arousal will be inter-preted as challenge and fun. Same arousal – just a dif-ferent interpretation. With enough confidence, anxiety is virtually non-existent. So...when confidence is greater than the threat = you get excitement and fun. When confidence less than the threat = you get fear and have a really lousy time. Simple.

(Performance Task + Risk)/ Confidence = Amount of Anxiety

Officially, as soon as we consciously notice physiological arousal associated with stress we call it, **Somatic Anxiety**. Worry, the spinning helpless concern about a future situation is called, **Cognitive Anxiety**. In a recent experiment using snakes, people were inca-pacitated by fear *only* when *both* somatic anxiety AND cognitive anxiety were at high levels. When cognitive anxiety was high and somatic was low, participants could still perform their task. When somatic anxiety was high and cognitive anxiety low, they could still perform the task. So we may need to redefine bravery in the future. Someone without any somatic or cognitive anxiety can't really be called brave. Or can they? Also, someone with incapacitating somatic and cognitive anxiety, to the point that his or her body no longer responds, can't really be called a coward. It doesn't take much to be brave when your body and mind aren't cranking out overpowering anxiety.

People who are confident about their ability to perform a task look at the shaking hands and pounding heart as excitement.

People actually look forward to arousal when they're confident about their task and ability. Bob Hope would bounce on his toes before entering stage. Boxers bounce around on the mat cranking up their arousal level. They do it because they unconsciously know they need to pump up the arousal level they need for the ring. Every individual and every different task has a particular arousal level that is right for them.

So, today, stage fright is generally considered have of three component parts:

1. Cognitive anxiety, or what we normally call *worry*.
2. Physiological arousal that we consciously notice (Somatic anxiety).
3. Confidence. (Confidence is a variable that changes the game because it changes our interpretation of situations.)

Cognitive anxiety, or worry, can start when you're about to perform something new and unfamiliar, something complicated, something important to your future, or something you haven't done in a long time. Many women take a break in their career to have a baby, for example. Coming back can be painful because of the wagonload of doubts coming from their imagination. They often fear that during their time off they somehow magically lost their performance ability. This simply isn't true. Though having a baby sometimes shifts priorities, it doesn't steal their performing ability. It's normal for the initial performances after a hiatus to be a little scary, but that's only just your imagination doing its thing.

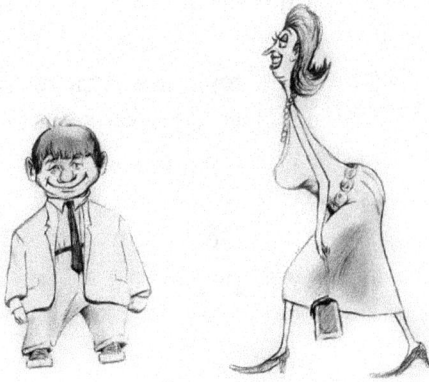

4. GENETICS AND ANXIETY: BLAME YOUR PARENTS

Genetic traits are also a part of the stage fright equation. Traits are permanent behaviors that distinguish us from others. In addition to genetic traits, we incorporate behaviors caused by incidents in our past. Many times, genetic traits can be hard to distinguish from acquired behaviors.

There are many tests that try to measure a person's trait personality. In most parts of the world, the Five Factor Model, or the Big Five, is the most accepted. Through factor analysis, personality was boiled down to five basic domains: Conscientiousness, Agreeableness, Neuroticism, Openness, and Extraversion. Temperament Scales, such as the Jungian-based Myer-Briggs, are still used, but are less academic. Still, temperament scales do provide useful information, helping to identify temperaments that fit certain careers. The MMPI is a terrific tool to measure traits, but it's long and intense...great way to spot psychopaths though.

Whether using the Big Five, MMPI, or a Temperament Scale, the most crucial information about stage fright comes from items that measure Neuroticism, Introversion, and Extraversion. Most of the time I'll try to refer to the Neuroticism scale as Emotional Stability, since that is it's current description. I also want to make it clear that Introversion is not the same as Neuroticism, even though they are related. There are plenty of emotionally unstable extraverts out there.

**Introverts are driven by a fear of punishment.
Extraverts are driven by rewards.**

The more emotionally unstable and introverted you are, the more a fear of punishment will motivate you. You'll probably anticipate failure more because you're hypersensitive to signs that equate to danger. The danger radar of the introvert is extremely sensitive. Introverts have a nose for danger. They go to great lengths to avoid it. They prepare for work earlier, stay longer, and avoid risks. They can learn to be outgoing, but it's not something that doesn't come naturally. They may gravitate to quieter jobs involving complex mental processing and do very well there. When walking into a quiet library or a museum, or talking about what sword you used in a role-playing game, experiences that might bore extraverts to tears, introverts feel right at home. Interestingly though, even though the neurological alarm systems of introverts turn on sooner than extraverts, their maximum arousal levels don't go any higher than those of extroverts. Introverts aren't cowards.

Extroverts are motivated by novelty and reward. They go after things because of something they want, or because they're bored and need some novelty. They don't look for, and therefore don't notice possible dangers as much as introverts. When they *do* notice possible dangers, they may not have a lot of fear. Consequences aren't as big a deal. Extroverts just don't worry a whole lot. They don't reflect as much on what they've done. They don't ruminate on the past as much and therefore don't get as depressed as introverts. Being in front of people is generally easier for them because mistakes don't tend to haunt them. They are less likely to develop cognitive loops of worry when performing. Since worry overtaxes the brain, extraverts may have more free processing space available when in front of an audience.

You'd think after my explanation, that only *extraverts* would want to perform in public. Not true at all. Performers are a mixed bag of personalities. Some of the greatest performers I've ever known, in various performance domains, are introverts. And make no mistake, extroverts experience stage fright too. They just have to be further outside their comfort zone.

Another way to look at introversion and extroversion is from the perspective of avoidance or approach. The introverted tend to avoid new situations that may hold dangers. The extroverted tend to approach new novel situations looking for rewards.

An additional perspective is that of activation and inhibition. A theory by Jeffrey Gray explains extroversion in terms of neurological systems. Extroverts pos-

sess a behavioral *activation* system (BAS), while introverts possess a behavioral *inhibition* system (BIS).
Those with an *activation* system have a need a lot of
fuel to feed their arousal furnace. These are the people
who walk into a noisy crowded nightclub and suddenly
feel great because they've finally got enough stimulation to satisfy their system. They seek environments
that appease their arousal hunger. Instead of distraction, arousal actually may help them concentrate. With
an inhibition system, introverts use the brake more than
the gas.

I'm explaining all this only to help you identify
your unique personality. Whether you're an introvert
or extrovert doesn't really matter, but it'll give you a
clue as to how much preparation you need, and how
much distraction you can take. It may also stop the
comparisons. You can't compare yourself to other performers because we each have unique traits that require
special handling. You may need more or less time during each stage of training. Introverts will usually rehearse longer and require a bit more time for the distraction phase of training in order to feel secure. Extraverts may not have as much trouble with distraction, but
they get bored easily. So don't compare. Just create a
process that works for you and stick to it.

No matter what your personality, confidence will
still be the one factor that determines how you interpret
each performance situation. Confidence affects introvert and extrovert alike. Shaking hands, sweaty palms,
the pounding heart are signs of adrenaline and cortisol.
When confidence levels are high, these substances are a
non-issue. When confidence is low, their presence

makes us more fearful.

Below is a test to determine whether you're an introvert or extravert. Answer with a "yes" or a "no" to each question. Add up the yes's and no's. The more "yes" answers you have, the more likely it is you are an introvert. The more "no" answers you have, the more likely it is you are an extravert.

INTROVERSION/EXTRAVERSION TEST

1. I'm a really good listener.
2. Others describe me as "easy-going" or "quiet".
3. I prefer to talk about meaningful things rather than frivolous things that don't matter.
4. It's easier to state my feelings when I write.
5. I don't like answering the phone.
6. I like doing one thing at a time.
7. During a project I don't like interruptions.
8. In a classroom, I normally don't raise my hand.
9. I tend to think before I open my mouth.
10. I don't like big loud parties.
11. I don't like taking risks.
12. I lose myself in whatever I'm doing and often don't realize time has gone by.
13. I like people but don't mind spending time alone.
14. Money was never a big motivator for me.
15. Being in big crowds wears me out.
16. I don't like showing people my work until it's completed.
17. I prefer parties where I can have conversations.
18. I avoid conflict whenever possible.
19. I like people, but often feel like an outsider.
20. I like quiet places where I can concentrate.

5. FEELING GOOD: ZONES OF EXCITEMENT

It's vitally important to understand that arousal; shaking hands, nausea, cold sweat, is not the enemy. It's all about how we LABEL that arousal.

We all have levels, or zones of arousal that work best for each thing we do. Football practice may be one zone, playing the actual game may be another. A rehearsal with orchestra may be one zone, performing with them in front of an audience would be another. Different zones work for different phases of a task. You look forward to high arousal before you run a race. If you're playing chess, operating on somebody's brain, or disassembling a bomb, your arousal zone should probably be low enough not to cause shaking.

When you learn to perform a task, it's important to put yourself into the proper zone of arousal, and condition that zone into your body. Top athletes instantly jump into the level of arousal that's best suited for their type of performance. They know instinctively where they need to be. Once you've made your task as automatic as you can, you owe it to yourself to practice in your performance arousal zone to condition your body to reach that level automatically.

I mentioned Bob Hope before, bouncing up and down on his toes before a performance. He unconsciously knew that he needed to be at a particular level of excitement before he went on stage. He took himself to that level without thinking about it. You'll see many athletes and entertainers revving themselves up before they run on the field, or onto stage. At the Winter Olympics, members of the US ski jumping team started hiring a guy named Pete Lavin to yell at them just before they go out the chute, working the athletes into a frenzy. His loud frightening voice helps them reach the high levels of arousal they need when they leave the chute.

Physically active tasks require a higher level of arousal. However, many stand-up comedians raise their level of arousal before entering the room too. They unconsciously know they need to *bring* energy into the room. Even those comedians who seem slow and relaxed on stage are at a higher arousal levels on stage than in everyday life. If you need more arousal, it's an easy fix. Run in place. Jump up and down. Shadow box. I knew one performer who played "Joe" in *Showboat,* who would shadow box right before his entrance onstage singing, "Old Man River". He'd go out, sing his song, get a standing ovation, then go back to his dressing room and read the newspaper.

When your zone of arousal is right, things fall into place. It won't be nervousness; it will be excitement. That's why I like to call them zones of *excitement* rather than zones of *arousal*. Performing should be exciting, or else why do it?

6. DISTRACTION: THE MIND ON OVERLOAD

Okay, let's get down to the nitty-gritty.

If your task requires a lot of concentration and/or the use of fine skeletomuscular movements, high arousal works against you. Arousal is distraction. Complex tasks are highly sensitive to distraction, whereas simple tasks, such as running or swimming are not. In fact, some athletic performance tasks seem impervious to any amount of distraction at all.

Let's say you are a locomotive. The train speeds along, then all of a sudden there are rocks all over the tracks. If the tracks are wide and straight, (automated

- confident) you may be okay, but if the tracks are narrow and shallow, the train may jump its tracks. The same thing happens to your performance. If sufficiently distracted, anyone can jump the tracks and end up on a different train of thought. Confidence and making the task automatic widens the rails so it's harder to jump the tracks.

Anthony Hopkins, when performing in *Equus*, forgot his lines when some people came into the theatre late. He had to ask for his line before he could continue. The famous operatic singer, Enzio Pinza, was singing an aria while someone in the front row was rocking to the music. He had to stop singing because the rocking was breaking his concentration. Studies have shown that air traffic controllers with as much as ten years experience can be distracted enough to forget a plane is on the runway.

Competence gives birth to confidence, and confidence helps to keep us from being distracted. Competence is generally the product of experience and successful past performances. There are, of course, individuals who don't care much about competence, and therefore aren't likely to suffer stage fright. They aren't worried about what people think. Some small percentage of the population will always have boundless confidence regardless of their ability. They self-promote with abandon and sadly enough, people believe them. While you're sitting around worrying about whether you're competent, these people are bragging their way right to the top. We don't know if they're delusional, narcissistic, or both, and I wish I could say they aren't successful. But I can't. They worry less, and therefore come across to the public as being more competent. Sociopaths fit in this category too, by the way.

Keep in mind that the more you examine what you've done, or what you're about to do, the less confident and assured you appear to be. Using past experience and imagining future outcomes is one thing, but obsessively ruminating about past failures or future dangers is another. If you've been success-ful in the past, there's usually no reason you can't be in the future. But you have to work at it.

For most of us, a feeling of competence is de-sired before we go into battle. Most of us want to know we're ready for the situation and that our per-formance will be at least what the situation requires. But to be competent, we have to be comfortable enough skill-wise to keep our attention in spite of distractions. If we focus on the distractions, our at-tention the task will suffer. Distraction can come from outside stimuli, disruptions in the performance, or our own interior thoughts. It can come when we notice our heart pounding, or our hands shaking. It can come in the form of sound, lights, a button miss-ing on a suit, a sore throat, a missing button, insects, or a question we weren't expecting from the audi-ence.

If your task is performed well, all negative future scenarios vanish.

If your performance is guaranteed to be perfect...threat can't exist. If there's no chance of embarrassment, no chance of losing a job, no danger of destroying your self-image, no possibility of ruining your public image...why would you have stage fright? So...with no possibility of a bad performance – you have no performance anxiety. Yet why is it we all tend to approach stage fright from perspective of the distraction, instead of the task! It's all about the task folks. If it goes well...so does everything else.

Worst-case scenarios only come true if we fail. So work hard to insure that you cannot fail. Generally, after you begin the performance distractions fade away because you're becoming more and more engaged in the task. Attention that was momentarily gobbled up by worry, is absorbed back into the task. Learn the task backwards and forwards. You may still be nervous, but you're a trained monkey. Go out, bang your cymbals, collect money in your little hat, and go home.

The purpose of distraction is to gobble up attention.

Distraction interferes with long-term memory retrieval. It may be that Eye Movement therapy (EMDR), the eye movement therapy reporting success in the area of Post Traumatic Stress Disorder (PTSD), works in the same way. Moving your eyes rapidly may upset memory retrieval, separating emotion from memory. During EMDR, while the client is moving their eyes rapidly to the right and left, they are asked to recall the traumatic event. In some cases the emotional memory of the event is greatly reduced afterward. It may be that eye movement, during the initial stage of recall, is a distraction that disconnects or interferes with memory retrieval, disconnecting memory from emotion. A similar effect is noticed with giving people small electric shocks while they are asked to retrieve memories.

Distraction will always exist in varying amounts. The only way to make it less distracting is to get used to it. If you add distraction to your training process, you can immunize yourself against it. If distraction succeeds in stealing away attention, don't fight it. Don't chase the distraction. That's like chasing your tail. Concentrate on the minute details of your task. Minute details will help you pull your attention away from the Dark Side.

7. RIPTIDES OF FEAR: SWIMMING SIDEWAYS

We may be overflowing with arousal before a performance event, but it takes cognitive anxiety to push in the clutch and start the gears of fear moving. The opposite seems to be true as well. Unless physiological arousal is added to cognitive anxiety, the performance generally continues unabated. So, if you're worrying (cognitive anxiety), but have no signs of physiological (somatic) anxiety, you'll probably be fine. And, if you have signs of somatic anxiety (shaking, sweating), but no cognitive anxiety, you'll be fine. It's when you have both high cognitive anxiety – AND – high somatic anxiety, that you may have a problem. One's okay – both are not. Got it?

Okay...we all have a tipping point where arousal is concerned. It's always one straw that breaks the camel's back and scatters attention to the wind. But...which straw? That's why stage fright is so difficult to predict. Our genetic background is one straw. Our past experiences...another straw. Watching other performers going on prior to us is another straw. Noticing our pounding heart and shaking hands is yet another. A difficult performing space may be another. These straws compound until they are too much for the camel. If you're right on the verge of this happening, turn into a machine. Think mechanically. Stage fright is best approached mechanically.

The normal reaction, when being pulled out to sea by a riptide, is to try to fight the current and swim straight back to shore. But riptides are too powerful and the more effort you spend fighting the current, the more tired you get, and the further you're taken out to sea. Swimming sideways to the riptide, however, is easier. Once you're out of range of the riptide you can easily swim to shore.

The crazy thoughts that come to mind about the performance being a catastrophe, the shaking, cold sweat, the zillions of fears attacking you from every direction...those things are like a powerful tide, taking you further and further away from your purpose. So start swimming sideways, regain control, and get back to what you're supposed to be doing. You *own* your task. It's yours. Check your engine. When the road gets bumpy drive more slowly and take control of the wheel. Don't try to "wow" anybody. Just stay on the road. That's all. That'll be enough.

Simplify, simplify, simplify.

Most of us are afraid of negative public opinion. Sure, it can be devastating and can result in real problems. If you are the dictator of a small unstable country, negative public opinion can be life threatening. Also, in many cases it's not just YOUR performance that's at stake. If you're on an Olympic relay team, or part of a Broadway cast, it's not abnormal to worry that everyone else is depending on *your* performance. Stage fright is a big mind game. It's a current of thoughts that pulls you out to sea.

Simple successful performances are better than spectacular failed performances.

Don't think you can talk yourself down. Anxiety isn't an acid trip; it's part of your neurological motherboard. It's a cognitive cake mix with dozens of ingredients, all hinging upon one thing – the future. And what does that scary future depend on? The performance. Where does the performance live? In the *now*. I know. Easier said than done. But pretend that every time you go into the future, I'm there to slap you silly. Believe it or not, that would help. Maybe you can pay somebody to do that?

If the performance is satisfactory, anxiety will just go POOF! Disappear. That's if it's just *satisfactory*. If it's *good,* or *great*, anxiety will be left even further in the dust. Trying to quash distraction is the wrong way to approach stage fright. Swim sideways by using short cuts to simplify the task until the fear of failing isn't so uncomfortable.

There will be times when no matter how well prepared you are you'll still feel nervous. Maybe because something in the environment is funky. Maybe something went on a minute ago that turned on your alarm systems and the bells are still ringing. This is called Excitation Transfer. Emotions from before, carry over into your next activity or thought. And even if you've performed a task a hundred times, weird little distractions may be enough to turn those alarm systems on. Happens to pros all the time and they just accept it as part of the job.

RULES OF THE GAME:

1. At times of high threat, simplify the task.
2. To best serve your audience, keep them separate from you and the performance.
   a. You can't anticipate what the audience is thinking. You don't read minds.
   b. Audiences want to feel good and they can't do that if you feel badly.
   c. You can't fix what you've done wrong during a performance. Don't overcompensate to make up for it. People have short memories. Just finish the performance competently and half the time they won't remember a thing.
   d. If you get distracted and go off the tracks, hook back up to the performance by cheating in any way possible to make yourself feel secure. Simplify to the point where you can once again control the task. Confidence will come back.

If you're a public speaker, don't feel weird about *reading* the speech. Don't feel weird about using a PowerPoint to cue your speech. If you're an actor, don't feel strange about leaving lines all over the floor, or on props. Some film and TV actors actually allow other actors to paste their lines onto their body.

In fact, some actors have earpieces, giving them the dialogue, because they're too lazy to learn their lines like everybody else. It's rude, but they do it.

In TV, actors can become very popular and begin to make more money on outside gigs than they do in the show. Or, they begin to take their job and the money for granted and get lazy. Success does that. Success can make us think it will last forever. So getting popular actors to rehearse can be difficult. Often cue cards are used so all the actor has to do is read their lines off a poster-sized card. This is regular practice on Saturday Night Live because there's no way they have time to memorize the lines. In the old days blackboards were used instead of cue cards. The point is, using gimmicks like cue cards, or earpieces, don't matter, obviously. They've been in use for years.

Obviously when you know the material, or when confidence is high, you can leave the gimmicks behind. But make it a rule, here and now, to stop putting yourself through grief trying to prove something that the audience doesn't give a damn about. Performance isn't a memory contest unless you're doing memory tricks. Getting the task done. How you do it doesn't matter as much. It's a job. Perform adequately, not brilliantly, just adequately, and none of your bad dreams will come true.

Everybody memorizes at different speeds. Again...performance is not a memory contest. Some Shakespearean actors or opera singers take a year to learn a role. Spend the time. If you're a singer and are worrying about the high note, choose a lower note. If you're an ice skater and haven't done the lift enough times to feel safe, don't do the lift, for God's sake. If you're a tennis player and you're not sure you can get the ball over the net with the speed you want, do it with less speed, but get it over the damn net. Simplify so you can get the task done. Doesn't have to be great or spectacular. You just have to get the job done.

When your confidence levels are high, it either means you're delusional, or you're feeling competent and confident about the performance. You have a high level of self-efficacy. When you're confident, you feel free to do anything you want. Go for greatness. In fact, when your confidence is high, you'll probably *add* distraction just to make things more exciting.

In long running shows on Broadway, the performers are doing all kinds of things that you, the audience, never see. During Evita, one friend of mine used to wear nothing under his coat and flash other cast members on stage. The actor, Bradley Whitford, remarked that while on stage each night doing *ART*, his co-star, Roger Bart (along with Michael O'Keefe) would look at him cross-eyed trying to make him laugh. Actors play tricks with props, change lines, stand where they aren't supposed to, make faces... This kind of stuff goes on constantly without the audience ever suspecting. Athletes, when they're bored or overconfident, run when they normally pass, shoot from half court, make up new plays, take chances where they normally wouldn't. People add distraction when they are comfortable and confident. They add distraction whenever they want to add excitement back into the performance. So distraction, like arousal, isn't a bad thing. It all depends on how much, and when.

Performers have the most fun when they know they can control the task completely. The ability to focus attention on the task is the primary result of confidence. If performing is torture it means the task holds too much danger potential. I can't make it more simple than that. You'll know you're in a good place when performing is just like brushing your teeth in the morning.

You will instantly know if you've removed enough threat from your performance, because a physical wash of relief will pour over your body. It's a physiological response when stress is relieved. Through the years as a hypnotherapist I've noticed that particular response happening over and over. A sigh and a physical wash of relief. If happened whenever I would hit upon a word or phrase that relieved a person's anxiety. The individual would take a breath, sigh, and their body would suddenly relax. Once the anxiety drops low enough, our ability to think on our feet returns. Then you can start adding back your personal nuances that make the performance yours again.

MORE STRESS – SIMPLIFY THE TASK.
NO STRESS – ADD TO THE TASK.

Stress is cumulative. How much stress a person can take is never truly predictable because we each have tipping points that lie below consciousness. Think of any performance as the fabric on a trampoline. When you've trained and have confidence in your performance, the fabric is firm and elastic. When there's too much stress, the fabric of the trampoline may give way unexpectedly. With training, even with moderate stress, automatic *chunked* behavior will keep the trampoline firm, letting us bounce around for a while even if our mind goes somewhere else. Performers rely on automatic behavior to take over when their mind wanders.

Imagine doing a 2-hour play filled with dialogue. An actor is often distracted... many times their brain goes blank. When the dialogue in on automatic, their mouth moves and the words continue. Imagine a 4-hour surgery. It's not abnormal for the mind to wander. As long as you don't panic, you'll find a cue from somewhere...maybe another actor's lines...someone handing you a scalpel, maybe from the look of things, or from your position on stage...and you'll get back on track. You should hear the laughter in the dressing rooms after and actor messes up or forgets a line. Nobody's immune to distraction, but when you train well and have control over the task, chunked automatic behavior can pull you through.

If you're afraid you'll forget the words, swim sideways and write them on the floor, on props, on your hand. If you're a public speaker, swim sideways and use PowerPoint or read your talk. If you're an ice skater with a partner, swim sideways and do the easier lift. Do whatever it takes to make you feel comfortable. Don't set yourself up to fail. Don't put yourself under stress. Why? Work things out ahead of time so that you can do a good job, good enough to not be embarrassing. A good performance will always allow you to walk away without regret. And once you relieve the stress you are free to be brilliant.

A good performance in times of stress is better than a brilliant performance that crashes and burns. The audience doesn't want to feel your discomfort. They want you to succeed. So do them a favor. Don't try to gain their approval. Swim sideways. Focus attention on the task and not the distraction. Use gimmicks and cheats. In the long run the people watching really don't care.

You see, challenges that are way beyond your ability are in fact, NOT challenges at all. Any gamer knows this. Anyone teaching sports or the arts knows this. If you're just learning to play the violin, picking a complicated piece is just plain self-destructive. It chips away at your confidence and sucks all the fun out of playing. But practicing an easier piece that's only slightly more difficult than your skill level offers a challenge and a reward. Success offers a neurological rush of pleasure. Winning results in an activation of the pleasure centers of the brain.

But there has to be the *chance of winning* before

we feel challenge. Without a good chance of winning the game isn't fun because there's no challenge. And challenge is a crucial ingredient of engagement and fun. Tasks that are way beyond your skill level are NOT helpful. So keep your goals just a bit passed your skill level and no more. Robert Browning was right when he wrote, "Ah, but a man's reach should exceed his grasp, or what's a heaven for?" We love challenges. Challenge is why we keep playing the game.

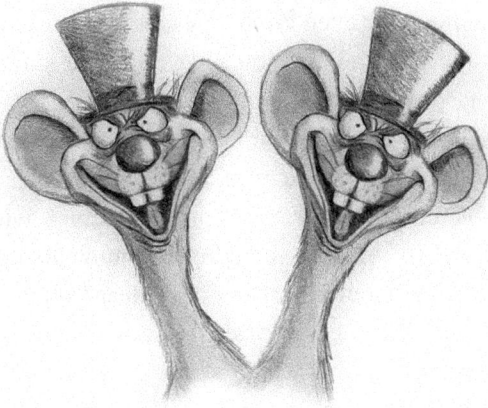

8. CHUNKING: ...AND THE TWO SHALL BE AS ONE...

Once you practice your task enough, smaller thoughts and movements start melding together to form larger more complete units of behavior. So a bunch of little pieces of the task melt into each other. Soon you don't have a bunch of little pieces, you have just a few big pieces. Instead of a hundred things to think of, you might have only three. Long-term potentiation occurs among the neurons in the brain when you repeat a behavior. They stay lit longer. When those neurons ignite again and again because you're repeating something, neurons adapt and store the memory. Soon motor neurons are being triggered automatically. Your task magically starts to occur without you consciously being involved.

It really is kind of magical. It's often such a

struggle getting a performance task off its feet. Imagine first learning the violin, or break-dancing, high jumping, or even typing. Tasks can be so grueling in the beginning. You have to make sure your finger is on the right string, make sure you get your legs over the bar, make sure your body weight is over your skates before you spin...and you do that over and over until you start doing those things without thinking. All the little thoughts and movements you used to think about separately have been automatized and chunked together. Instead of thinking about all the movements necessary to shoot a bow and arrow, you just think about the target. Everything else is automatic.

Zen masters made this process seem mysterious by using beautiful, yet vague poetry. But it's really an amazingly organic process. Here's how to do it:

1. Practice the performance task. Just practice the basics of the task repeatedly. No thinking about when it's going to end. No worrying about the future.

2. If the performance task is lengthy, break it into sections and practice each section. But finish the whole task during each practice session. Keep concerns about the end result out of your head. Just repetition.

3. If you practice the task in sections, you'll begin to notice that some sections are pulling together and becoming automatic. When enough sections of your task are automatic (you can perform them without consciously controlling them) start prac-

ticing the task as a whole, in logical order. If there is no logical order, create some logical order, no matter how ridiculous. Our brain needs some order, some kind of logic in order to make sense of what you're doing.

4. Set aside time to practice parts of the task that are slow to chunk. Once these parts join the rest, and become automatic, practice the entire task as a unit.

5. Now add emotion. Add different kinds of emotion, to the task. Perform parts of the task angry, sad, or happy. You can name the sections. If you're a pole-vaulter, in the running section you can be "the Flash"; during the launching into the air section you can be "Superman" and so on. Giving names to each section of the task can help retention and make things a bit more fun. Be excited, funny, or hyper. Make up moods to use while practicing. It sounds crazy, but adding emotions to your performance will help it chunk and reduce the number of pieces.

Finally, your task will have been chunked into just a few units that don't take much conscious control. It doesn't have tiny individual pieces anymore. Human brains *love* to generalize and condense. We can compact a lot of information and behavior if we just practice enough to allow our brain to chunk things together.

For example, I spoke to one of the cast members touring in a show called, *Altar Boys*, once about their choreography. They only had three days of rehearsal and I wondered how they put the dance sections up so quickly. He explained that each of the dance sections had a name. One section was called the Brittany Spears section, and each of the other sections had names too. Instead of hundreds of individual movements to remember, they chunked them into dance sections named after famous performers.

You owe it to yourself to have fun when you perform. Your best chance of having fun is to make the performance something you can perform any time, any place. Make things automatic, leaving as much room in your head as possible for the *WAY* you want to perform instead of *HOW* to perform it. When the task is chunked and automatic, your mind is free to do other things, able to concentrate and focus on the *way* you perform it. That's when it belongs to you.

9. CONFIDENCE: THE MAGIC FEATHER

In the classic Disney story of Dumbo, a baby elephant had ears so large he was able to fly. But even though Dumbo had the ability to fly, he was too afraid to take to the air until he was given a magic feather. The feather wasn't magical of course, but faith in its power gave him the confidence to try.

Confidence is faith, faith that our performance will be successful. We've all heard of the placebo effect. About as many people given medication for depression improve when they are given a placebo, as they do when given prescription medication. Placebos work because of faith. It's an age-old concept and the reason witch doctors still exist in many forms today. Confidence affects what we do in the present, because we have faith that we can't lose.

There are two elements of confidence that affect performance.

1. Faith in our training and control of the task.

2. Faith that what we do will satisfy *OUR* expectations, and the expectations of the *AUDIENCE*.

A professor of Asian studies at UCLA, talked to me once about an ancient Japanese training manual he was translating. It was an instruction manual for teachers of Japanese princes. The instructions stressed that a prince must never know fear. A prince must never know defeat. The theory was, if a prince doesn't *know* fear or defeat, he'll assume victory is the only possible result. That can also be delusional...but hey.

Fears are often conditioned. A few episodes of anxiety before performing and you've already set up a pattern. However, if we are conditioned *into* doing something...we can condition ourselves *out* of doing something too. It takes time and training, but it can definitely be done. Generally it means that you have to start with ridiculously simple tasks in front of an audience, simple enough that there is absolutely nothing you can do wrong. No threat. Performing without threat will extinguish the old responses and replace it with new ones, but it will take a number of performances to accomplish this.

Train without worrying about the end result (assume you'll get where you need to be by following your training plan). Use repetition until your task is automatic, or at least as automatic as it's going to get. Perform in public again and again so that you can get used to distractions and disruptions. Facing distraction time and again, lessens our fear of it. Remember that there are no perfect performances, just unique ones. Plus, we know that mistakes increase our desire to be correct...so you have that going for you too.

We learned during the self-esteem movement, that confidence doesn't come from wishful thinking or chanting. It takes proof. It takes real, honest-to-goodness work, and clumsy performances are part of that work. No one wants to look like an idiot. When a performance goes wonky, yeah, it's fearful and embarrassing. However, the fear of embarrassment is also a fuel. It's creates emotion and motivation to speed up learning. We've all had experiences in school when we didn't know the answer to a question, or gave the wrong answer and looked like an idiot. Not wanting to look foolish is a major motivator. Many a Broadway show is in tatters before previews, but, since no performer wants to look like a fool, they work like crazy and miraculously pull it together at the last minute. Ice skaters, dancers, gymnasts, public speakers, and all performance domains benefit from mistakes, because embarrassment promotes learning and negative reinforcement.

Okay, what's negative reinforcement?

It's very misunderstood. It sounds like it would be punishment, like getting an electric shock every time you do something wrong. Actually, negative reinforcement is what you do to *prevent* the electric shock. Embarrassment is what you want to avoid, so negative reinforcement is the training you do to avoid it. Whatever you do to avoid something negative, is negative reinforcement. Negative reinforcement is a good thing unless taken to the extreme. If you're well prepared, there comes a point when preparation starts to give you diminishing returns. The idea is to make the task as automatic as possible. Once you do that, obsessively practicing is overkill and will make you resent the task.

Training is like putting yourself on a conveyor belt. The task starts out on the conveyor belt in pieces and gets dumped out on the other end in the form of automatic behavior. When the conveyor belt dumps you out on the other side, it's usable, finished, and you can mold and shape your performance the way you want it.

You ever notice that when someone reaches out to shake hands, you automatically do the same? We're conditioned to do this. We don't think. You done it so many times you're now conditioned to do it. You'd be surprised to learn how *much* of your behavior is automatic. This is why behaviorists had such a stranglehold on psychology for so many years. A lot of what they said was true. We want to be unique and creative, but that freedom comes from not having to think about how to mechanically perform your task, so that you can think about the *WAY* you perform your task. Conditioning works. It works for Olympic athletes, politicians, scientists, singers, public speakers, parrots, and penguins. It's simple. It's not rocket science. Yes, it can be really really boring. But it's a facet of training you can't skip. And...it builds confidence in your training process, which becomes your magic feather.

Mistakes are part of the process and because you don't want to be miserable and anxiety-ridden, you'll take actions (negative reinforcement) to prevent mistakes. Every performer makes mistakes. And few audience members remember mistakes. If you trip, if your mind goes blank, join the club. It's part of being a performer. Glitches are a part of performing.

Again, audiences have short memories, folks. Social psychologists and advertising executives have known this a long time. It used to be that if someone did something socially unacceptable they were ostracized. But with the advent of modern instantaneous media, we know that humans have very short memories. New information floods in and replaces old information. Fame and infamy *both* create celebrity. Humans are fickle. Performers need fans, but they also rely on audiences to be fickle. So if a performance crashes, remember: the public has lousy long-term memory. Perform well next time, and they'll love you next time. You're giving the public a lot more credit than they're do. When you're up there in front of an audience, they assume you belong there.

If you're a novice and you make a mistake or screw up a performance, you're lucky. Think what it's like for veteran performers who make mistakes. When *they* make mistakes it can make them question their whole life, their whole purpose on the Earth! It makes them wonder why they've wasted all the sacrifice and training. The more you invest in your career as a performer, the more you expect from your performance.

Confidence is all about the springs...

Confidence is an example of Hooke's Law of elasticity – it's all about the springs. If your performance is a trampoline...the elasticity of the trampoline comes from the springs attached to the fabric. When you're confident and in control, the springs will always support you. Even if your performance is difficult (heavy), even if there are important people in the audience, even if it is vitally important; if the springs are strong you'll be perfectly fine and still have fun.

If the springs are NOT strong, elasticity will be low, triggering evolutionary survival alarm systems setting off high physiological arousal. A lot of cognitive capacity might be taken up with worry. Distraction can become a weight the springs can't handle and instead of bouncing, you hit the ground.

The stronger the springs are, the greater your confidence, and confidence interprets the whole performance situation. The more threatening the performance - the stronger those springs *have* to be. When our public and self-image is threatened it's like putting a 400lb gymnast on the trampoline! But if the springs are strong, you still have no worries.

If the situation looks like a failure waiting to happen, bow out, or renegotiate your performance agreement. Explain that you didn't agree to these conditions and if you do perform, it will be under a different agreement. Change the performance to match the conditions. If you're on a team and feel you're on an equal playing field with other athletes...then you might go ahead. But don't set yourself up to fail.

If you *do* make a mistake, you'll learn from it. Don't beat yourself up because moods are very sticky. They stick inside your head. So don't let them get in there in the first place. If you're feeling like a failure, kick that feeling's ass. I mean it. And not tomorrow. Today. That minute. Kick it right out of your head. Don't give it any time at all to get comfortable. It's your imagination turned to the dark side. Treat your ability – your body and mind – like a valuable, efficient machine. Negative voices are like putting rocks on the railroad track.

Everybody has moods. They're pretty harmless. But long-term they're not good. Negative moods can be like bad rainy weather. Let it go on long enough and your machinery gets rusty. Put a tarp over your brain in foul moody weather. Close your eyes and keep walking forward. It'll be okay. Goals in life often appear hopeless. Doesn't mean you won't get there.

Yes. There are times when you have to face facts. You might want to rethink your goal if you expect to be a 70-year-old prima ballerina. You might not want to set your sights on becoming an NBA player if you're under 5 feet tall. But in most cases, you're body and brain aren't that much different than anybody else's. If someone else can do it, so can you. Be patient. Be consistent.

Ignore voices in your head that tell you it's hopeless. Everyone hears those voices from time to time. Star performers aren't immune to the voices. I've worked with plenty of them. But the faster you kick those useless negative thoughts in the teeth the better. You'll get where you're going, don't worry. While no one can guarantee fame or fortune, even a rat can learn to do tricks. The only difference between humans and rats is: Rats don't worry.

10. THE AUDIENCE: WHO ARE THESE GUYS?

Social scientists have been studying the effects of
audiences for over a hundred years. Surprisingly, we
haven't found out a whole lot. This is primarily because we can't experiment with humans the way we
experiment with rats. People would complain.

In the early 20th century, human thought was considered to be metaphysical mumbo jumbo, like talking
to spirits. It was only after World War II that we really
started to measure human thought. Then the behaviorists took over the psychological world, and human
thought was thrown out the window once more. Behaviorists strongly believed everything was stimulus and
response. And a great many things can be treated this
way, learning especially. It works terrifically on animals, but with primates hmmm...not always. Humans
kept doing things they weren't conditioned to do. It
frustrated the hell out of behaviorists who wanted to

break down all behavior into some mathematical equation. There was something humans had that other animals didn't, and that *something* made them behave in unpredictable ways. This *something* is our larger frontal cortex. It was *thought*. Our ability to imagine, our ability to retrieve historical events and build imaginary futures. That ability changes what we do. So, in the late 1950's, the importance of human thought in performance once again gained attention.

The behavior of all animals changes when they are around others of their own kind. It doesn't matter if you're a human or a walrus. Some changes are positive and aid in performing a task. Some are negative and get in the way of the task. The effects of the *presence of others* depends on what <u>kind</u> of *presence* we're talking about. Here's what we know so far:

1. Having other people around who are performing our same task (co-actors, competitors) tends to improve our performance. When performing the same task as other performers (like a bicycle race), those competitors usually make the task easier and helps us perform better.

2. Having other people around who are performing a *different* task than us, doesn't affect us much at all, unless they are abnormally disruptive with sound, physical interference, or visually distracting stimuli.

3. Having other people watching us while we're performing a *simple task* tends to help our performance. It bumps up our arousal level and, speeds up our reactions. We go into a higher gear. But the task has to be simple.

4. Having other people watching us while we're performing a *complex task* tends to hurt our performance. Complicated tasks are fragile and sensitive to stress. Stress threatens complicated tasks and kicks in our flight or flight system, stealing cognitive ability. A chess player, a neurosurgeon, a physicist, would have a more difficult performing their task in front of others, than say, a house painter or a long-distance runner.

5. An audience of experts creates more stress than an audience of non-experts because the performer knows for sure the performance is going to be judged. (Stage fright is all about being judged.)

6. Small audiences can create more stress than big audiences because it takes more energy to get them engaged. Most often adjudicators, experts, or judges are small audiences. Small audiences can be more stressful than large ones.

The size of the audience is counterintuitive. That's why auditions tend to be more stressful for musicians, dancers, actors, and singers than actual performances. The threat potential is high. But remember that these "experts" don't want you to fail. I've listened to the conversations of expert judges for years, and all they talk about are the people who gave them a thrill and who made their day a bit brighter. They want you to be good and enjoy yourself. That way they can relax.

Big audiences are subject to behavioral cues; so many times a big audience is easier to please. We're a bit like lemmings in some respects, we clap when others clap, we yell when others yell, we're quiet when everyone else goes quiet, etc. Big audiences follow cues better than small ones, like schools of fish, or herds of wildebeests. Somebody starts clapping in a big audience and it catches on quickly. It only takes the movement of 3% to 5% of the herd to turn it in any direction.

Years ago, Robert Zajonc, though a brilliant scientist, proposed that the mere presence of other humans caused arousal, yes, simply by having bodies in the room. Hmmm...

Now, as brilliant as he was, obviously wasn't a performer. The theory never had effects large enough for it to be fully accepted, and there was a reason why. An audience of blindfolded, ear-muffed people isn't going to threaten anybody. Brainless zombies wouldn't bother a performance either, although the smell might be distracting.

I say this to people all the time, "There is no stage fright in an empty room." What we fear is the negative *judgment* of others. Stage fright is all about judgment, or at least it starts out that way. When we imagine an audience making negative judgments about us, *or* when we are judging ourselves negatively, threat jumps through the roof. It's all imaginary, but our body and mind react as though a tiger just walked into the room.

It's not a crazy cowardly thing to be afraid of what an audience is thinking. Let's face it, the judgment of an audience can indeed affect a person's income, career, and self-worth. It's not something to be taken lightly. Our brain associates the negative judgment of an audience with real physical threat because... sometimes it IS a real threat.

But here's the truth about audiences....

No audience wants to see you fail. Even experts.

Audiences come to see you out of need. They *need* entertainment. They need to be inspired. They don't come to see you fail. Yes, some *competitors* might love to see you fail. But an audience never wants you to go down in flames.

Why?

There is a part of our brain dedicated to feeling the emotions of others. We broadly call the process "empathy". Actually, mirror neurons are activated when we watch others. We see an accident, see people in anguish, and we subtly mirror their grief by activating those same muscles in our own bodies. How many times have you cried when watching a movie, or when someone else is in tears? Mirror neurons cause your body to feel what someone else is feeling...or what you imagine they're thinking. It's a bit more involved than that, but you understand what I mean.

Audiences don't want to feel your pain.

Audiences don't want you to feel badly; producers and directors don't want you to feel badly; test examiners don't want you to feel badly; most bosses (other than those who have power needs) don't want you to feel badly. No audience wants you to go down in flames unless it's professional wrestling.

So, if you're auditioning, remind yourself *none* of

those people sitting behind the table want you to fail or to be embarrassed. It would be uncomfortable for them. They want to have a good day. They want to do what they came to do, then have a nice lunch. They don't want to have to say, "Don't worry about it. Those things happen" in some attempt to make you feel better. It never actually makes people feel better anyway. When you fail, they feel yucky too. Trust me!

You don't have to knock their socks off. Just do a good job. You may get hired because of your looks, or the way you sound, or because you're tall, or because you look like somebody's aunt. There is any number of reasons for choosing someone other than talent or skill. They may not need a great performance in order to hire you. If you *can* be spectacular – by all means *do so*. But in most cases you only have to be competent. Go in, do a good job on the audition, the test, or the athletic preliminary rounds, and go home. Nobody's out to get you. They actually *want* you to be good and have a good time.

Most performers blame themselves when they are not chosen. (Actually, people who blame everybody else for their problems tend to be physically healthier...go figure.) Performers train so hard they become myopic. In their mind, everything comes down to talent and ability. But there's more to it. Other factors often influence people's judgment as they watch you, plus or minus. And those things you can't control. So, just do a good job. You may not score the best time; you may not jump the best distance, but if you do a good job at least you can always go home without embarrassment.

Self-image is easily damaged when a performance goes wrong in public. Most performers put in years of sacrifice and training. Imagine what it's like to suddenly believe it was all for nothing, that everything you believed yourself to be is a lie. That's a lot of pressure.

Pressure and stress from our own fears of being a failure is one of the major causes of stage fright.

The fact is, you're going to trip or fall sometimes as a performer. People who are in the spotlight *risk* embarrassment. Performance is all about *risk*. And you, as a performer, live with risk all the time. It's the cereal you eat for breakfast. You live with levels of risk that would make non-performers melt. Just another day for you. If you trip and fall...what are you going to do? Become a librarian? Probably not. You're a performer. Slipping and falling is how you learned. Your journey was built on mistakes because mistakes made you learn faster. That's the secret you can use. Mistakes speed up learning. The best of the best make performance mistakes. Perfection doesn't exist.

11. THE BIRTH OF THE FOURTH WALL

A lot of stuff happened at the end of the 18th century. For one thing, it was the beginning of the end for the agrarian society. Workers used to be hired to do a job and were paid at the end of the job. They took breaks, talked as they worked, and took days or weeks off after the job was completed.

Then the machines came.

The machines in the cities needed workers to feed them, so agricultural workers moved from rural areas into highly populated areas. Companies pared down the work force to the cheapest, most pliable and complacent workers – usually women, children, and immigrants. Salaries were disgustingly low and a typical workday could last 18 hours. Women and children were often abused by their superiors, but never reported the abuse because their families couldn't survive without their meager salary. The machines ran day and night, never done, on and on, endlessly. Suddenly, jobs had no end. Machines needed to be fed day and night. So, wages switched from being job-based - to being hourly-based.

Out of the industrial revolution arose an elite upper class in the United States, something that arguably hadn't existed up to that point. These were the newly rich, the industrialists like the Rockefellers, Carnegies, or Vanderbilt's, who created dynasties in the coming years. The new upper class had a number of pastimes, primarily horse racing, theatre, long vacations, and philanthropic projects such as parks and museums. Their wealth separated them from the herd. They had celebrity. They were envied. Their lifestyle was so different from the herd that a psychological distance separated them from the lower economic classes. They lost their ability to imagine how hard it was to live at a subsistence level.

Because of the extreme differences in lifestyles, the rich naturally felt more comfortable surrounded by their own kind, and gave the poor a wide berth. Distance from the masses became something synonymous with the rich. Distance gave them a new perspective. They began to give distance to performers as well. They created space between themselves and athletes, actors, singers, musicians, artists, and dancers, setting them apart, and by doing so, they inadvertently granted them respect.

This was a bigger deal than you might think.

For centuries, performers were very close to the audience. Too close in fact. In the old days, female actors were regularly groped, actors had to watch for flying objects, fist fights broke out...I know... good times...good times... In fact, when professional prize fights took place, the audience often broke into fights themselves. Races were regularly interrupted by bystanders who became so emotionally involved they attacked the contestants. Performances were only surface deep, because the performers always had to keep one eye out to protect themselves from the audience. It's awfully hard to focus when you're worried about a bottle flying at your face, or a hand reaching up your skirt. Once the rich gave performers their distance, performers finally felt safe enough to fully concentrate on their task. Without distraction from an audience, performers where set free to truly perform.

This was the birth of the Fourth Wall, a revolution in the performing arts. It was around this same time that Stanislavski developed his "system" of acting. But distance wasn't just given to actors; it was also given to dancers, singers, acrobats, and any number of performing domains. Still, it was in the domain of acting that changed most dramatically (pardon the pun). Actors were finally able to move from melodrama to psychological realism. They finally had the luxury of imagining their character's feelings and surroundings. They were able to enter alternate imaginary worlds.

At the same time, the industrial revolution was finally paying off by boosting the economy, creating a middle class. Workers had extra money with which to enjoy leisure pursuits.

Which pursuits did they pick?

The middle class gravitated to the pursuits of those people they envied...the rich. So the middle class also began granting distance to human performance too. The fourth wall became unanimously adopted. This helped both the performers and the audience.

Why is the fourth wall so important?

Because the fourth wall creates an agreed-upon invisible shield, protecting the performer from the audience. The fourth wall creates an *empty room* for the performer, like a force field, keeping the audience out, allowing the performer to fully concentrate on their task.

Is it fair to keep the audience out?

It is more than fair, it is essential. In order to truly give your all to an audience, you have to be 100% on your game. The fourth wall helps you do this by creating a safety shield. Then when other performers join in that imaginary world, magic occurs. By having the freedom to concentrate, a performance is more complete, more impactful, more exciting, because there's no tiger in the room. No one interferes with the race. For actors this was an incredible leap forward. For the audience too...because *the further actors enter their unreal worlds on stage, the more real the performance seems for the audience.*

So, yes, it IS fair to keep the audience out. In fact, keeping the audience out, separating them from the performance, is the best favor you can grant them.

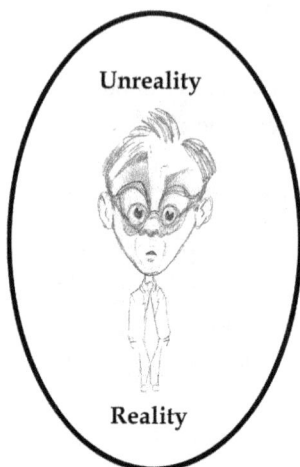

12. CLUB MEMBERSHIP: THE AUDIENCE ISN'T A MEMBER

The only difference between a crowded auditorium and an empty room is you, imagining someone is going to think badly of your performance. Noise, movement, technical difficulties, and worrying about what the audience is thinking, can cause enough distraction to trigger our defense mechanisms.

I'll talk more about it later...but even though the audience is what scares us...it's not the audience that is the danger. *What we're really afraid of is that we'll ruin our performance.* A bad performance gets a negative evaluation from the audience, right? But if we're confident our performance is going to be great, the audience holds no danger at all. Social science labels stage fright as *evaluation apprehension.* But that evaluation is about the performance. If the performance is fine, everything else is fine.

The audience has a psychology all its own. While an audience is made up of individuals with individual wants and needs, an audience also becomes a single entity run by Groupthink. They follow the responses of the herd. They are there to experience something interesting, unique, and exciting - as a fan – as a connoisseur – or as a voyeur. If we worry about what's going on in their heads it steals from them. That is why, as much as the audience may *want* to be a part of the performance, you owe it to them to keep them out of it.

Performers belong to an exclusive club and the audience is not a member!

We only have so much attention to go around. If a performance is fraught with anxiety, it means our brain is in danger of being overloaded as we desperately try to process all possible negative future scenarios. In order to prevent a negative outcome, we start to monitor everything we do in the smallest detail. Micromanaging a performance is really expensive. It pulls apart all those tasks we worked so hard to chunk and automate   Micro-managing causes us to consciously control every little particle of the task separately. So basically, we're back to square one.

When a computer's processing power is used up, the system freezes. Often, you have to reboot to get started again. That's pretty much what it takes with the human brain when your performance breaks. You have to reboot.   Once stage fright breaks a performance, arousal may have to drop all the way back to zero before it can be restarted.

So don't do that, okay? Promise?

Don't even get started in that direction. It's stupid.

Kick the audience off the stage, off the field, and out of your head. When you're doing your task, you, or you and your team, are the *only* members of the club. You don't have to imagine the audience naked (although no one can stop you). All you have to do is put up the fourth wall and do what you've trained yourself to do. Be the trained rat. Stop being so conceited. The world doesn't revolve around you. Do your job and go home.

If you've put your task through an adequate training process you're ready to perform. Training works. Training has worked for thousands of years. The procedure isn't painless of course. It can be grueling. It can be boring. But training and conditioning go hand in hand with how our brain works. The only thing that can screw up that natural process is if you let the audience in. On the field, in the ring, or at the podium, the performance belongs to you and NOT to them. They can drool and wish they were you – but no matter how much they wish, it's not going to happen.

I keep repeating this. You have to understand that you as a public speaker, actor, dancer, athlete, politician, musician, enter a very exclusive club. Not many people choose to perform because they don't want to work that hard. Even if performing fell into your lap, you're still a member of a very exclusive club. You pay dues to belong to that club. The audience doesn't get to be a member. And that fact makes what you do even more appealing to them.

They don't have a card, or a key, or a password.

They may inspire your performance. The cheers may bump up your arousal levels and make you run faster, or have more fun. They may be so engaged in your performance that you're able to do things you've never done (all performers know that audiences give off a palpable energy). They may provide perks, fans may want to sleep with you, or take pictures with you, or endorse their products, but they still don't get to be on stage, on the field, in the arena, or in your head. And if you let them in there...you're cheating them.

You practice, practice, practice until your task gets as automatic as possible. You target troublesome areas of the performance that need more help, focusing your rehearsal. You add distraction to cement the perform- ance and to build immunity from distraction. That's your job. The audience doesn't pay those dues. They don't get to be in your head. Period.

That Fourth Wall is there for a reason. Use it.

Do this and your brain will have all the room it needs to play. You can have fun. You can add more and more nuance, personality, and timing to your per- formance. You can notice the needs of the audience more. You can steer the performance the direction of the audience and put your twist on each movement or decision you make. If things get too boring, add a little more distraction and liven things up.

Attention is like a precious metal. Wasting it on the audience is like using gold to make paper clips.

Attention is a commodity. Corporations spend hundreds of millions of dollars a year trying to get your attention so that you'll buy their products. And you're *giving* it away? Come on!

Wasting ANY of your valuable attention on what the audience may be thinking is a sin for a performer. THOU SHALT NOT SIN. Serve your audience by keeping them away from your performance. The less you think about them, the more they'll think of you. Weird huh?

I can't tell you how many people have told me, "...and whenever I don't care if I win, whenever I just enjoy what I'm doing, I do great!" Why? Because once we stop performing for others, we have no physiological or cognitive inhibitions. We're free. We can be ourselves. Why perform at all, if you can't be yourself doing it? Try to be what the audience wants and you stop being you - then what's the point of performing. The audience should never own the performance. They wouldn't know what to do with it.

Here's another thing: For years I've watched novice performers try to *get the audience on their side*. They pose, gesture, add cute tricks, fake smiles...they act like the tough guy, act coy, act like the rebel, swagger, snub...not knowing that it's all a waste. It's energy wasted unless that stuff aids your performance. It also looks fake. The only way to truly get the audience *on your side* is to be good and sincere at what you do.

Performers who don't pose, don't gesture, don't even smile, but who just pour their heart into their task...the audience *loves* those guys. Some of the finest actors in history have been those who simply don't care if you like them. They don't give the audience, even the director *anything*. They do what they think is right for the character. Oddly enough, not caring about the audience makes your performance more real. If your skill or craft isn't enough, all the posturing in the world isn't going to save you. So be your best self. Win or lose, that's all you've got, baby.

Love your task more than you fear criticism.

I sang the funeral of a beloved football coach at USC. One former member of the team went on to play pro ball, and remembered a time when he was injured during a game. He was injured while he was grand-standing, playing to the crowd. The coach flew to that city, walked into his hospital room, pointed a finger at the player and said, "Don't you be a fake, you son of a bitch! Don't be like those other guys! Don't you be a liar!"

The player knew exactly what he meant. He knew coach was telling him he had gotten caught up in the money and the celebrity of the national leagues. While playing for USC, the coach had taught that player to play from the heart, for the game, to be a true warrior. He was telling him he had become a mercenary of the public.

This is a lesson to all performers in every field of human performance. Be true to your skill, your train-ing, and your craft. When you perform for any other reason, you're a fake.

13. PRACTICING: THE PERFORMANCE ON AUTOPILOT

Repetition is our friend. I use chess players as an example because it's a game where players are so stereotyped. We all have this image of them as quiet, moody, intelligent nerds. But chess players aren't that much more intelligent than anybody else...and rarely are chess players geniuses. The fact is, highly success-ful chess players are simply people who have played so much chess, that they no longer have to *think* about playing it. I know that sounds crazy, but it's quite true. When you repeat ANYTHING enough, it reduces the amount you have to think. That's why surgeons, when *they* have to have surgery, pick a the surgeon who's performed the most procedures. When we do things often enough, things become automatic. We start run-ning on intuition, rather than conscious thought. Our work becomes magic.

We may have a little better understanding of how this happens now, thanks to a high functioning autistic savant, a man in Scandinavia with unprecedented recall abilities. He is able to describe the inner workings of conscious thought for a savant. He can add huge sums of numbers, can become fluent in a language in a week, demonstrates all sorts of miraculous mental feats with little effort. He describes seeing numbers and sums of numbers, as patterns of colors. Totals to an astronomical stack of figures shows up in his mind as a unique pattern of colors. His brain somehow translates this unique combination of colors as a number. What is to the rest of us a Herculean task, to him is as simple as describing a picture.

Every big task is made up of a lot of little pieces, like a jigsaw puzzle. A golf swing, a football pass, a tennis serve, a triple jump, are all made up of thousands of unconscious signals and muscle movements. In the beginning we concentrate on controlling each of these commands and muscle movements, but after we've performed the task over and over and over, our brain starts remembering them and making them automatic, chunking those pieces together. Like the autistic savant, we begin to treat the task as a single task, a picture, with all the little pieces automatically taking care of themselves.

Fewer parts....less thinking.

The idea is to memorize beyond the point where thought is necessary, memorizing to the point of *automation*. And if emotion and meaning are added to the process, automation will take place even faster. It would be great if we could just take a pill and skip the time it takes to automate our task, but alas, it doesn't work that way. Most things worth doing, take time and effort. That's an old trite saying, but it's true. Since most people aren't willing to put in that time and effort, they come to watch those who ARE willing.

I've run into a lot of artists and creative types who are afraid of the word "automatic". Some are even afraid of the word *rehearsal,* fearing it will steal their spontaneity. What can I say? That's just garbage. Lawrence Olivier once stated that he could never improvise until he had completely memorized his lines. Candidates for political office memorize their speeches thoroughly before they feel comfortable going off script to answer creatively. Even improvisation troupes have to memorize and practice basic improv rules and structure of the scene, before they can "make things up".

Get the mechanics out of the way so you can start enjoying what you do.

Suffice it to say that there are many locations within the brain responsible for memory. We now think individual neurons throughout the brain store share parts of a memory. So memory is scattered all over the brain. However, the area generally responsible for converting short-term into long-term memory is the hippocampus. Short-term events stimulate one set of neurons within the hippocampus, which stimulate another unique type of neurons that actually change shape. So when neurons are hit hard or repeatedly, they become easy to excite the next time. They remember their excited state.

It was thought that during sleep we solidify memory, the things we learned that day. What actually happens is that all the little things that surround a big event, tend to fade away. Memory of the big thing stays. It seems to be remember better because all the other distracting memories around it faded during the night. Sleep clears away the clutter and makes the big things stand out.

When the stimuli coming into the hippocampus is intense enough, a wave effect occurs. It's an intense event like a storm that sends waves of impulses, battering the shore, each successive wave adding to the effect on neurons down the line. The longer that emotional storm lasts, the greater chance the event has of becoming etched in our long-term memory. In addition, smaller surrounding stimuli are often scooped up with the big stuff. That's why after catastrophic events, smells, sounds, even aspects of light can trigger traumatic memories. Repetition helps create long-term memory, but adding emotion to the rehearsal process may help create a wave effect to speed up the process.

Intense events can become long-term memories instantaneously. This is what happens with post-traumatic stress disorder (PTSD). PTSD is like an old plastic phonograph record, where the needle has been shoved down into the plastic really really hard. Then, whenever you put the needle on the record it skips into that deep groove you've made. With PTSD, the neurons storing the catastrophic memory have been conditioned to be easily excitable. They are so easy to excite that, once triggered, the painful crippling memories are nearly impossible to control.

Emotion, *even if it is pretend emotion,* will help you memorize. It makes the groove deeper so that it's easier to find the next time. The rehearsal process can be shortened if you *care* about your topic. Even if you *pretend* you care about your topic. As soon as we *care* about a subject it stops being boring. This goes for any subject you are studying. Caring makes things sticky. It helps make the task stick in your brain.

You want your subject matter to be as sticky as possible. Caring makes things sticky by giving them some emotional meaning.

1. We are meaning-making machines.

2. We seek meaning like the roots of trees seek water. We will seek meaning even if we have to make that meaning up.

3. Emotion adds meaning to things and makes them easier to care about, even if that emotion is pretend.

Emotion always wins over logic. A well-known soap opera director was asked if people believe the ridiculous plots that they have in soaps. He said, "If the audience tries to make sense of a soap, I haven't done my job". His job is to fill up each episode with so much emotion, no one notices the stupid plot. Most of our decisions are emotional ones. Might as well use emotion to our advantage.

Expect that insecurities will pop up during the rehearsal process. It's just good ole' cognitive anxiety.

Even the most practiced professional has fears about forgetting their lines, wondering if they've still "got it", wondering if the task is beyond them. All that stuff is the normal and I have to remind professionals of this all the time. Also remember that each person learns at different speeds. Automation WILL happen eventually. You'll get there. Just keep plodding along.

Training is the ugly side of performance, the boring, grueling part. But it's the only road to competence. <u>Very</u> few performers enjoy rehearsing when they are alone. It's lonely, frustrating, and tedious. Rehearsing with others can be fun because it's social, but even group tasks require individual training. Most professional athletes, dancers, singers, actors, or public speakers can't wait to get passed the training stage and onto the performing stage. Things start to get fun when you can actually play the game and have a good chance of winning.

14. CONTROL: THE SECRET INGREDIENT

Performances don't have to be brilliant. That's the first thing to get out of your head. Most performers do their best simply because they don't want to feel their life is being spent doing something mediocre. Sure, we want to be brilliant at all times, but in most cases, performances are simply rehearsed tasks that go according to plan. Performing is a job. It doesn't have to be great to be called a performance. It just has to be *on purpose*. It has to *not* be an accident. It has to be in your control.

Fear occurs when you believe the task in out of your control. If your performance is out of control, your chance of making a mistake is high. It's like Russian roulette. That's a game that makes most people nervous. For most of us...the odds aren't good enough to want to play Russian roulette. We don't have enough control to make it fun or safe. If you know you can absolutely control the task, it means you can pretty much guarantee your performance will be acceptable.

In every machine, that part that has the greatest

flexibility will be the controlling part. Flexibility implies choice. If everything is on automatic, it allows your brain the freedom to make choices *while* you're performing. It allows you to tilt and shape the performance. Having control is what allows you to be an artist. It doesn't matter if you're a sculptor or a heavy equipment operator. Even within a company, the person who can make the most decisive choices affects the company the most. So...the most flexible performer will affect the audience the most, because they realize its not about "wowing" the audience...it's about shaping the performance.

There are only a few rules to remember when you're seeking to be in the driver's seat of your performance.

1. The training process should become a religious ritual. The process works. Have faith in it. Follow the training ritual and you'll always come out okay.

2. No audience comes to a performance wanting to see you fail.

3. Not every performance you give will be great. Every famous politician, singer, dancer, musician, and comedian has wonky days. Just be competent.

4. Measure every new situation's threat potential on a scale of 1 – 10. In threat situations over 7, cut your performance down to its most basic form. Use performance aids, cue cards, slides, films, and recordings, wear special braces, teeth guards, use medication if you absolutely need to.

5. In threat situations under 3, increase the complexity so that you don't get bored.

When threat it high, use as many gimmicks as possible so that you don't feel you're walking a tightrope without a net. Reduce the risk. It's not cheating. It's common sense. Plus... NOBODY CARES! How do you think gymnasts learn to do back flips? They use pullies and trampolines to them get used to doing flips. That's all you're doing when you use gimmicks, or notes, or slides, or a stool, or a ladder, or a wheel chair. These are merely ways to make tasks easier. It's not a lie. Use films, slide presentations, volunteers from the audience, backup singers and dancers, rely on teammates or cast members. Create a safety harness whenever you lack the confidence to perform the task competently. Aids like this add additional stimuli. Aids take a load off your shoulders. They help you get to the point where they are no longer needed.

We get used to things.

We can get used to winning.

We can get used to losing.

We can get used to earning a lot of money.

We can get used to earning just a little.

We can get used to being happy.

We can get used to being miserable.

I've known people who got comfortable making truckloads of money effortlessly, and thought it will last forever. It got boring so they started to sabotage it. They succeeded.

I've known performers who got comfortable performing brilliantly, never having had a performance go terribly wrong. Then, when a performance *did* go wrong, their anxiety snowballed out of control to the

point that they stopped performing entirely.
Don't do that. It's stupid.

Get used to completing your task competently using whatever tools or gimmicks that give you control over the performance.

Put in the time. As things become automatic, target your practice. Once the entire task becomes one chunk, add distraction to cement your new automatic behavior.

15. PERFECTION: THE MYTH

We spend a lifetime building our self-image, or self-concept, our brand. It is a construction of the things we want to be. Most of the time we want our self-image to match our public-image. If we fail in public, both our self-image AND our public image take a hit. They're tied together. When they don't match, a dissonance occurs between who we *think* we are, and who we *really* are. That cognitive dissonance is unbearable. Even the *fear* of this dissonance can cause stage fright.

Here's the thing...self and public images are artificial constructs. We'd like to believe they're permanent, but they aren't. Our thoughts and actions can stray from our constructed image at any time. We're not perfect. We sometimes do things we're not proud of. And that causes dissonance.

We aren't designed to be perfect. We're designed to be flexible. Performances are never perfect. All performances are unique. Your goal in a performance of any task is NOT to make it perfect. Just the way you want it.

True perfectionists rarely complete anything, because after the first tiny mistake the performance is no longer perfect. So they quit.

It's the imperfections that give us identity. Quirky people are easily remembered. Perfect people don't have imperfections or quirks, so their personalities don't stick out. Both a perfect personality, and a perfect performance are forgettable, because they contain no unique memorable qualities. They become a ride, like at Disneyland. Imperfections and quirks give us something to hold on to, something to remember. A bowling ball, for example, has three holes in it. How would do you hold on to a bowling ball if it was a perfect ball? Perfection isn't all it's cracked up to be.

If you get anything out of this book, make it this: Your ideal performance is one that accomplishes your goal —one that contains your unique personality. Otherwise, let a machine do it.

When you are confident in your ability, you will always let your imperfections become part of the task. Every imperfection helps people remember you. The quirks and imperfections within your performance can actually become the secret to your success.

It doesn't matter what you wear, or if every hair is in place. If your performance is excellent, and if it's unique, people will remember you. In fact, they'll adore you for being unique even if the performance is just "good". We humans are attracted to unique. Don't for a second think that you need to be perfect. If you drop that aspect of performing, it will change your life. Never envy another performer's style. They are colleagues not competitors. Even in sports we are only competing with ourselves. As Oscar Wilde once said, "Be yourself. Everybody else is taken."

16. TRAINING: DESIGNING YOUR OWN TRAINING PROCESS

Many readers may have skipped right to this chapter because this is the heart of the book. So, let's get down to it...

Training involves operant conditioning, a fancy way of describing how an elephant is trained to stand on its hind legs and wave. During this process you're training yourself to perform a task while becoming immune to distraction. Your goal is to automate your task as much as possible, and then flood yourself with distraction over and over while you perform it. Then you're ready.

Imagine a cat who's deathly afraid of dogs. Put the cat in a room for days and days, surrounded by dogs, all barking hysterically. Make sure nothing threatening happens to the cat – pretty soon, the cat's alarm systems start to re-adjust. The cat's natural alarm systems stop going off. The cat eventually *learns* to ignore the dogs. Re-adjusting alarm systems is the one thing missing in most training programs.

Here is the order of your training process:

1. PRACTICE WITH THE GOAL OF AUTOMATING THE TASK.

2. AS PEICES OF THE TASK BECOME AUTO-MATIC, TARGET YOUR PRACTICE TO THOSE AREAS NOT YET AUTOMATIC.

3. ADD EMOTION TO THE TASK EVEN IF IT FEELS LIKE PRETENDING.

4. ADD DISTRACTION TO THE PERFORMANCE.

1. **Set aside enough time to train.** Repetition is your friend. The longer you have to train, the less likely you will be to develop anxiety. Automatic behavior is referred to as "dominant behavior". When we're learning new behavior, stress causes us to pop back into our most familiar dominant behavior. Once a new behavior becomes dominant, it takes the place of the old dominant behavior. It's like recording sound on an old audiotape. The new sound goes on top of the old sound. The more complicated the task, the more work it takes to make it dominant. So, obviously, every task requires different amounts of training. Running

and jumping is behavior that's already pretty dominant already. Skills can be tweaked, making you better and better, AND physical conditioning should be maintained. If you're training for a speech, give yourself at least two weeks. If it's a very familiar subject, you may only need a day. Broadway performers have 6 to 10 weeks for rehearsals. Dancers have very short rehearsal periods. Shakespearean actors may work on a role for a year. It all depends on your task. Opera singers take years to learn roles, but they may have to fly in and perform those roles with only a few days of rehearsal. This causes a lot of stress, and explains why many opera stars use beta-blockers. Musicians, especially symphony soloists, have many constraints that cause stress: everything has to be exact. This amounts to a lot of stress. The shorter the training period and/or the more important the performance, the more potential anxiety exists...for anybody, not just you. Decide how long each day you need to practice and stick to that schedule. Rehearsing is your job. There is a point of diminishing returns, so don't be obsessive about rehearsing. Six hours a day practicing the violin is very likely to burn you out and ruin the enjoyment of playing. Think of how much time per day you will need in order to make that task comfortable to perform. That time becomes your rehearsal schedule. Stick to the schedule. Make it reasonable. Make a *reasonable* schedule that will allow you to learn your task.

2. **Target your practice to stubborn areas.** As you practice bits and pieces of the task will begin to lump together into memorized chunks.

The parts that don't chunk together are begging for more attention. So target your practice, giving stubborn areas of the task more time. Still practice the entire task as a whole, but lay aside time for stubborn areas until those areas become chunked with the rest of the task. Your goal is to be able to perform the task without thinking. In some performance domains that's impossible, but it should still be the ultimate goal of your process.

3. **Give your training periods as much respect as the performance.** Training is work. It takes dedication. It can be exhausting. It can be boring. It is a sacrifice made for your particular craft, and that sacrifice is what distinguishes you from the audience. The training period should be respected. Remember: Much of your confidence will come from your faith in your training. Make the training reasonable and complete. Practicing your task should be like practicing religion. The sacrifices of a strict religion tend to make people more loyal to it.

4. **Give parts of your task an identity.** If you play an instrument, give sections of the piece a name and personality. If you're a public speaker, or a dancer, give sections of your material a purpose, a point you're trying to make. If you're a martial artist, make up imaginary opponents. If you are a singer, make up the story you're trying to tell with the song. If you're an actor, make up the staging. All this adds emotion and identity to parts of your task, increasing the possibility that you'll remember it.

5. **Recognize and compliment yourself when parts of the task become automatic. Throw a party**. You need free up processing space, just like a computer. Making your task automatic saves it to the hard drive, leaving your working memory (like ram memory) free. Anything you can do to free up memory will help you handle spontaneous needs that pop up during a performance. Athletes don't need as much cognitive processing to perform their task as say...a physicist. Simple tasks require less cognitive control than complex tasks. Arousal helps simple tasks, but hurts complex tasks. Although athletic skills involve hundreds or thousands of tiny movements, repetitive training can chunk all those separate movements into one thought. The more familiar the material, the less time it takes to make it automatic, so parts of your task you've performed before will take less time to learn. That's the only advantage professionals have over novices. Experienced dancers, for example, have sets of movements already chunked, already named, making new routines easier to learn, the same for the martial arts. If the task is completely new, professionals have no advantage. Conditioning is conditioning. Training is training. It's the great equalizer. Professional or novice, we all have our own unique speed at which we learn.

6. **Add emotion**. Sometimes we have to perform tasks that don't really interest us. *Pretend* they do. We have different types of memory. *Explicit memory* is our memory of facts and events that are consciously retrieved. *Semantic memory* attaches meaning to those facts. *Im-*

plicit memories seem to come out of nowhere and involve very little conscious retrieval. With repetition, your task can become *implicit* over time. The different types of memory are like layers of an onion. The more layers we can involve, the more solid our material will be. *Emotion keeps things from being boring.* Inject emotion, or even fake emotion, into your performance whenever possible. It aids the memory process. Make your performance reek with emotion.

7. **Add distraction.** Distraction can come in the form of sound, sight, touch, or all three. To add distraction, wear earphones and play music with lyrics, or just use spoken words. Our brain is distracted by words more than music. Increase the volume as you become more secure. Add additional movement to your task as a form of distraction. If you can juggle or dance, do that too. Ultimately using friends to distract you is the most efficient method. This goes for all performers, musicians, athletes, public speakers, gamers...the more distraction you can flood yourself with, the better, and the faster you will become immune to distraction. Friends, who hit you with soft pillows, throw harmless objects, yell at you, flash bright lights at you, can speed up the distraction phase enormously. The extra *effort* needed to maintain focus during distraction, helps embed the task in your memory and conditions you into the habit of focusing on the task and excluding everything else. It immunizes your thoughts against distraction so that no matter what happens during a performance, your attention will remain undisturbed.

8. **Put up the Fourth Wall**. Watchers are not part of your club. You are the performer. They are the watchers. You are a member of an exclusive club of performers. They are not. They have no permission to be in your head because they haven't earned the right. If you find they are there, in your head, kindly eject them. They don't have a membership card. Your audience needs to be separated from you. You give better performances when they're separate. The fourth wall is a barrier between you and the audience, allowing you to supremely focus on your task. That focus is what the audience came to see. The fourth wall creates a safety zone, allowing you concentrate on your task. A feeling of control over the task is everything to a performer. You can't control what other people think, so you cannot include them in your performance. Keep the audience off the field, off the stage, and out of your head. You'll give a better performance, and they'll love you for it.

9. **Perform your task successfully four times in a row after distraction has been introduced.** Then you can consider your preparation complete. If not, keep practicing.

10. **Booster sessions.** Booster sessions will be necessary to keep your memory of the task from decaying. Over time, conditioned behavior decays, and reverts to older, dominant well-learned behavior. Booster sessions will prevent this decay from happening. So, set aside time everyday, or every other day, to practice your task. Again, add emotion to the task whenever possible. If it's a speech you're performing, be angry, or comic, or frightened as you give it,

just to add *play* to the task. Don't let the task become boring. If you're a pole-vaulter, pretend you're a superhero as you practice.

17. COMMON QUESTIONS

"So what if I can't remove distraction from a situation?"

Answer: Impossible. Let's say you're a smoker. If I snuck into your house late at night wearing a ski mask, put a gun to your head and demanded that you stop smoking, promised that I'd return in two months and kill you if you haven't stopped....think you'd stop smoking? This is why I keep telling people, "There is no such thing as will power." It's all about *motive*. Fears assemble themselves according to priority. Small fears can disappear in a puff of smoke when faced with a greater fear. If your confidence is low and importance of the task high, you need to use gimmicks to help, or you need to simplify and reduce the task requirements so that your confidence rises. If performing is painful something is wrong. Either you haven't trained well enough, or the performance environment holds too many unknowns. Fix the problem. If other people can perform comfortably, so can you. Take away any possibility that bad things that can happen, and "POOF" no more fear. Examine the situation, find the areas of threat, and fix them.

Yes, you may have a genetic makeup that is more sensitive to threat. That only means that you require more practice and more immunization from distraction than other people. You need more preparation and more control over the situation. What's wrong with that? Plenty of professional performers are just like you.

Don't worry about making the performance great. Just give a good performance, and use any kind of help you need to get that done. We give great performances when we are free from worry. Use whatever tools you need to reduce the worry. Use slides, use friends to prompt you, or literally read your speech off a sheet of paper.

Don't leave the distraction phase of your training until you feel like you're impervious to bullets and able to leap tall buildings in a single bound. If you're free from threat, the audience will enjoy your performance a lot more.

"What if I can't seem to shake the stage fright?"

That's not possible. Given the right training environment anyone can be desensitized to any stimulus. You just haven't flooded yourself with enough of the fearful or distracting stimuli for long enough. You may need additional training periods on the field or at the location of the event. Take away all the unknowns. Put safety nets all over the place.

When Patrick Stewart first started doing his one-man show, A Christmas Carol, he had little notes placed all over the stage. When his friend, Roger Rees, watched the show Patrick asked if there was something he could do to improve it. Roger basically said, "Yes, you can get rid of those bothersome bits of paper lying around everywhere." So Patrick drove his car up to Northern California and back, memorizing the script.

Amazing amounts of material can be memorized if you put in the time. Rely on your basic equipment. You have a nervous system that can be reprogrammed. If you've ever had deep massage, you know that deeply (and painfully) massaging a muscle that is in spasm results in the muscle and nerves becoming rather numb. We can do the same thing to our nervous system. Bombarding it with distracting stimuli will eventually result in it becoming...well, *numb* to that stimuli.

If your arousal gets too bad, and if the performance is vitally important to your income or self-image, go ahead and try beta-blockers. Beta-blockers have a side effect that not many physicians mention. It may reduce cognitive functioning. Don't be afraid of using them, but don't rely on them either. Go to Section Two and learn to find your baseline. That will tell you along about your unique wiring and how threatening a new situation may be.

Also, somatic anxiety, (i.e. a pounding heart, shaking, sweating palms, even nausea) is not bad. It's only bad if your level of confidence translates those symptoms as fear rather than excitement. When you're really excited, you can have the same symptoms. Remember: arousal itself isn't a bad thing.

If you can, practice at the event location prior to the performance. Take away as many surprises as possible. Simplify the task and use every gimmick possible. You'll know if you've reached the point where you're confident when you get a feeling like air being let out of a balloon. People generally let out an unconscious sigh. Anxiety is a form of pressure. We sigh when that pressure is released.

"I can't stand the idea of being in front of people."

You have social anxiety. You're probably introverted to the point where social anxiety overwhelms you. No problem. A lot of performers are introverts. It's very likely you haven't experienced a proper training environment. So you became convinced it was your fault. It's not. You may be more sensitive to threat. Just make the task simpler. Swim sideways. Don't fight the riptide of fear, simplify the task, until it's controllable, and your confidence will rise. Once your confidence is up, arousal will be translated as excitement. Find situations, classes or whatever, that allow you to get up in front of a audience. As you get used to having an audience, increase the complexity or your tasks.

"I have no fear of being in front of an audience. Can I reduce the training process?"

Short answer: Yes. But the fear of social judgment is just one tiny aspect of performing. *Automating* the task is the main purpose of training. Even if the task is automated and chunked, and even if audiences hold no threat to you, you still have to graduate from training by successfully performing your task four times in a row with distraction. I've seen a lot of confident people get over-confident and fall flat during their performance.

"I'm a public speaker who has given presentations for years. I should have confidence by now, but it never comes. I still feel like my whole life is on the line when I get up to present. What do I do?"

I've met several famous performers who say they're uncontrollably nervous just before they go out on stage. It seems to be part of their process. They do fine once on stage, so I think that they've gotten used to being nervous before they perform. Make a point to check yourself during the middle of your performance. Are you nervous? If not, chances are you're conditioned to be nervous right before you begin. You can condition yourself out of it. Have somebody do crazy stuff to you before you go out to distract you or make you laugh. Performing should not be painful. Or give the audience a task when you first go out. That gets you through the beginning of the performance without doing anything yourself. Also, what you're experiencing may be an unreasonable fear left over from some situation in the past. We never know what things are going to stick to the walls in our head. It may even be a product of childhood. If you remember anything about being in front of people from your childhood, what would that be? Were you nervous then? It's obvious that you have been successful at public speaking, since you're still doing it. You are successful in spite of your anxiety. No reason that won't always be the case. Do some digging. You've paid your dues. You deserve to have some fun in front of people.

"As a concert pianist I used to take beta-blockers. I still perform, just not as often. Is it a bad thing to take beta-blockers at this point since I'm not performing as much?"

Actually, you might want to take beta-blockers BECAUSE you're not performing as much. Beta-blockers prevent the production of adrenaline. They work rather well, and musicians playing in major symphonies around the world, particularly soloists, commonly use beta-blockers.

In the old days, alcohol was the drug of choice for social inhibition, or stage fright. Alcohol reduces executive decision-making and blocks one's ability to concentrate on consequences. You don't realize what you're doing is embarrassing, thus eliminating worry and guilt. So it does work, but only for a short time, then more alcohol is needed, then more, then more, and before you know it, you're an alcoholic. Many English actors were famous alcoholics. It's a form of self-medication that has destroyed millions of lives and has long-term effects on an individual's cognitive function. The side effects of alcohol make it a dirty bomb. The fallout is often worse than the explosion.

Beta-blockers are a cleaner method of eliminating the symptoms of stage fright (pounding heart, shaking). Due to the fact that you used it in the past, you probably have faith that it works. Faith in your process is a big part of confidence. I only care about what works.

Since you're not taking it often, I'd keep using it and experiment with smaller and smaller doses.

"I'm a teenager just beginning a career as an entertainer. I like being in front of people and singing. How do I make sure I never get started having stage fright experiences?"

There's no way to make sure. Stage fright pops up out of nowhere. Most entertainers have stage fright experiences at some time or other. It doesn't mean anything. Things throw us every now and again. Once when I was really young I went to see Sammy Davis Jr. perform. He stopped dead in the middle of a song when someone in the audience yelled, "I love you, Sammy!" He laughed and asked, "Where was I?" The musical director shouted out his place in the song, and he went right on.

We can't get rid of our imagination, nor would we want to. Stage fright is our imagination gone crazy. The same thing that makes us fabulous performers - makes us obsess over some possible negative future event. Performing should be joyous. You'll have ups and downs like everybody else. But without those things there's nothing to laugh about in the dressing room or locker room.

STAGE FRIGHT = DISTRACTION + THREAT/ SKILL AND ABILITY X CONFIDENCE

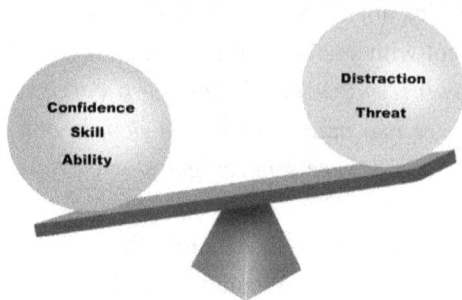

It's like a teeter-totter. As long as the teeter-totter is tipped in the direction of confidence, your performance should be fine. When it's not you'll feel threatened. Reduce the distraction and threat and the confidence side rises. Use gimmicks and tricks, tools that help you perform the task. Tip the teeter-totter in the confidence direction. Don't focus on the distraction, that's like swimming against the current. Distraction's not a variable you can control. Swim sideways. Concentrate on the task using tools or gimmicks to help you. Reduce the threat, increase control, and confidence will rise.

There are unforeseen events that occur during most performances, that's normal, and even fun. They are bumps in the road, but your hours of practice and experience provides the springs that smooth out the ride.

Distraction be made harmless by flooding, systematically desensitizing yourself to that distraction. It takes a bit of time. During the Civil War (although many lost some of their hearing) artillerymen eventually got used to the cannon fire. We can train ourselves to get used to almost any distraction if we have the time to do it.

Train yourself to react differently to distraction and threat. They are *"things"*. They are *illusions*. They are a trick the fools your brain. Treat your body and mind like a machine. Do what you have to do to make the machine work properly. Don't get all emotional about it, or catastrophize, moaning about how you'll never be able to beat it. There's nothing to "beat". It's a mechanical thing. Stop making it so personal. Be a mechanic. Find the problem and remove the threat from the engine. Improve your performance constantly. Impressing an audience is just a side effect of your overwhelming desire to surpass your own record. Put up your 4th wall and keep the audience away from your performance. Ironically, the audience will love you for it.

Some performances will be brilliant. Some will be just competent. It would be great if all your performances were brilliant. Some of you suffering from delusions may believe you are always brilliant. For the rest of us poor slobs (including the top performers in every performance domain) performances will vary.

Design your training so that you can trust it. Make it complete enough so that when you've completed your training you'll be ready for anything. Trust your training procedure. Use any help that you need to reduce that anxiety. Swim sideways and focus on the task, not the outcome. Automate the task so that you'll be free enough to improvise. Even when your heart is pounding and your hands are shaking you can be having fun.

Performing is part of life. It's as natural as breathing. If it's not like that for you, it can be.

PART TWO

18. ANXIETY: TAKE YOUR PERFORMANCE TEMPERATURE

What's the current amount of anxiety? On a scale of 1 – 10 (10 being that your heart is about to explode and your body and brain are about to catch on fire.) What is your anxiety level?

Current Anxiety Rating Scale

0   1   2   3   4   5   6   7   8   9   10

Anything lower than 6 is manageable especially for an athlete. It's basically just adrenaline you're feeling, and that won't kill you. Swim sideways. Don't fight the current by trying to ignore the anxiety. **Attention is the thing that's being stolen.** Point your attention at the task. When the task goes well, so does everything else. Focus on the task.

Introvert or Extrovert

$$\longleftrightarrow$$

1 2 3 4 5 6 7 8 9 10 11 12 13 14 15 16 17 18 19 20

Are you an introvert or an extravert? Go to page 19 and add up the number of questions to which you answer, "yes" and how many you answer, "no". If the majority of your answers are "yes" (over 13), you're an introvert. If the majority of your answers are "no" (over 13), you're and extravert. Introverts have to work harder than extroverts to feel calm and in control. Their genetic threat radar is more sensitive. Plenty of professional performers are introverts, so don't worry. Over time and with repetition, that radar becomes desensitized. We can *condition ourselves* to comfortably perform in front of people. It takes time, a training process that you trust, and being in that kind of performing situation over and over. If you only perform once or twice a year, there's no time to re-condition your threat radar. Don't put yourself in a situation like that. It takes time to feel comfortable performing a task. If you don't have the time, remove risk by using performance aids, gimmicks, and helpers.

With enough time, we can train ourselves to do almost anything. We're like performing monkeys with a bigger brain. So don't get too full of yourself. There are emotional, physical, and cognitive limitations, but in general, it's about training and desensitizing your threat radar. New situations may still throw you though...even if you're a pro. It happens.

Confidence Level

| 0 | 1 | 2 | 3 | 4 | 5 | 6 | 7 | 8 | 9 | 10 |

Close your eyes and imagine a scale from 0 to 10 and measure your confidence in regarding the upcoming performance. Anything below a 6 should indicate a need to shore up your performance with performance aids, cues that will make the task easier.

THE AUDIENCE DOESN'T CARE!

Audiences only care about a competent performance. Performing should be natural and well within your capabilities. When it's not...fix it. Add helpers that will make the performing situation easier. Don't live with anxiety. Performing is a challenge, like a video game. You can challenge yourself to do a better job every single time. If it's painful...something is out of whack. There's a threat somewhere. You're afraid you're not good enough, or there's too much distraction in the environment, or there's too much at stake. Remove the possibilities of a bad performance so that your confidence level goes up. Read your presentation instead of memorizing it. Drive slower around the turns of the racetrack. Don't pass the basketball as much. Pre-record your song and lip sync. Set up things so that the threat of something going wrong drops away.

Anxiety and confidence are negatively correlated. That means high confidence exists when there is low anxiety. Low confidence exists where there is high anxiety. Confidence levels determine how we *interpret* arousal. Low confidence interprets arousal (shaking hands, nausea, cold sweats) as fear. High confidence will interpret those same symptoms as excitement instead of threat. When your confidence is high, you can face distracting environments and tackle complicated tasks without feeling threatened. When your confidence is low, anxiety uses up a lot of mental processing power. With complicated tasks a cluttered brain is a problem, because you really *need* that mental processing power. Here's what to do:

1. Eliminate as many unknowns as possible.
2. Visit the site where you'll be performing, and run through your task as many times as possible.
3. Walk the paths you'll take to enter and exit.
4. Your performance should be like an old hat, something you've put on a million times, and something you can put on any time you want it.

5. Go through the task you're about to perform in your mind...go through the whole thing in detail. Visualize it from start to finish. Visualize things going wrong, holes in the track, strings breaking on your violin, your music stand falling over, snakes on the stage while you dance, etc. As that crazy stuff is going on, see yourself maintaining control. No matter what comes at you, you keep rolling along giving an unflustered, competent performance. ADD PERFORMANCE AIDS, CHEATS, NOTES, SLIDES - CUT CORNERS - TAKE THE CURVE WIDER - PASS INSTEAD OF SHOOT.
6. Do whatever it takes to get the comfort back.

Don't try for a great performance. Do your job and go home. It may turn out to be great. Trying for great performances often ruins the possibility of giving one. Good IS great when you're in a situation that's challenging. When things are wild and unpredictable, simplify the task until you feel in control. Add cheats (in a good way) and gimmicks to help you. We're not talking about performance enhancing drugs, or oxygenizing your blood here. We're talking about cheats and gimmicks that relieve any possibility of the performance going wrong. It's like adding bumpers to the side of a bowling alley so the ball stays in the lane. Put up the bumpers. When you've made it simple enough you'll immediately feel an immediate physical rush of relief. This rush of relief always happens when anxiety is lifted from the body. It's a very obvious physical sensation that you will recognize.

Performers on Broadway learn right away that the audience doesn't really notice too much. Understudies often go on before they know the staging or lyrics, and the audience is fairly oblivious. Performers learn to do their best and go home. It's a job. Like ice skaters, high jumpers, and baseball players, you train, combine that training with natural talent, and do what you're trained to do. If you make mistakes, you won't die. Your career won't be ruined. The public has a short memory.

19. REBOOT THE SYSTEM: FIND YOUR AROUSAL BASELINE

When we're highly aroused, adrenaline and cortisol are dumped into our system, preparing us for strength and speed. Systems in the brain needed for focused attention are shut down. If you're performing a task that involves attention, you'll need to overcome the adrenaline effects.

The following is a form of hypnosis. Even today, we don't understand exactly how hypnosis works. There are two basic theories, but you don't need to know that. All you need to know is that we enter trance states thousands of times a day without knowing it. You need to know that you can always reject any suggestion that goes against your moral belief structures. It's not Voodoo or black magic. It's just a way of relaxing, focusing attention, and getting passed thoughts like, "Gee this is stupid", so that suggestions stick.

Practice the steps below so that you can repeat the process anytime, anywhere.

BASELINE SESSION

1. Roll your eyes as far back into your head as you can.
2. Count slowly to 20. You're object is to fatigue the eye muscles.
3. Close your eyes and take a deep breath. Concentrate on relaxing your eyelids to the point that they don't want to open. As you release the air, blow out all the anxiety you have about the upcoming performance. Shake your body to shake it off if need be.
4. Once the anxiety is out of your body it can't come back.
5. Continue concentrating on relaxing the eyelids so much that they don't want to open.
6. On the back of your eyelids see the words, "To do my best for the audience, I keep them out." Repeat that quietly, mouthing the words.
7. Put up your fourth wall. See the wall, made of impervious bricks. The bricks will be invisible to you, but will keep away any threat from the judgment of the audience. With the audience gone, you will be able to give your best performance.
8. Count your breathing. Very slowly breath in counting to five. Breath out counting to five. Do this several times. Stage fright is a feeling of being out of control. By controlling anything, even something as simple as your breathing, you'll be re-installing a feeling of control.

9. Your back should be straight and you should continue to concentrate on keeping your eyelids so relaxed they don't want to open.
10. When you're ready, count to 20 and open your eyes, remembering that the anxiety can't get back into your body. No matter what happens, it can't come back in.

Test your anxiety level again. If it's still too high, go through the same rebooting process again.

Your imagination can change autonomic processes in your body. That's how anxiety gets started in the first place. Your human ability to imagine got you into stage fright, why not let it get you out of it!

Believe me, this process works. The more you practice this Baseline Session, the more quickly you'll be able to reach your baseline before a performance.

Imagine a Tyrannosaurus Rex walking up to you just as you're about to perform. If you don't feel any arousal, you're probably ready. It will feel very strange at first to perform without fear, with complete concentration on your task. It also feels pretty great. Performing is a fun challenge each time you get to see if you can perform even better than you did before. You're competing against yourself like in a video game.

The actor, Richard Dreyfuss, after receiving medication for his bipolar disorder, told his psychiatrist he felt unusually brave. His doctor responded (and I'm paraphrasing all this) that it wasn't bravery at all; he was just free from fear for the first time in his adult life. The removal of fear SEEMS like bravery, but it isn't. It just frees you to be you.

DON'T TRY TO CONTROL DISTRACTIONS!

When distractions occur stay with the material or the task. If you absolutely own the task you're performing, none of those scary things will come true. Don't get caught in the riptide of distractions. Swim sideways. Focus attention on the task.

DON'T BE AFRAID TO GET PHYSICAL

Trying to ignore your anxiety can sometimes multiply the effects of the adrenaline surge. Don't be afraid to work off the excess arousal by running around the block, or jumping up and down, or shadow boxing, push-ups, etc. Controlling your body makes you consciously realize that you ARE in control. When you're anxious, gaining control over ANYTHING is encouraging. Plus - physical activity can burn off excess adrenaline if you've got the time and the environment to allow for it.

What's your Performance Arousal Zone?

| 0 | 1 | 2 | 3 | 4 | 5 | 6 | 7 | 8 | 9 | 10 |

We have zones of arousal that work for different performing situations. What level of arousal do you need for the type of task you're performing? A 2? A 9? Sometimes performing in front of a crowd takes a higher level of arousal than you normally use. If you need a 7 and you're at level 4, you'll need to rev up for the task. Jump up and down, or shadow box. If you're at an 8, but need to be at 4, you'd better calm down. Do a Baseline Session. Do whatever it takes to get yourself to the proper level. Being above or below your performance arousal level will be uncomfortable.

20. ENGAGEMENT: THINKING WITHOUT THINKING

All performance tasks suffer by thinking about the end result.

Evolutionarily speaking, we were not meant to think so much. People who ruminate tend to be unhappier than people who don't. Preparing for most performances doesn't take a lot of thought. It takes a lot of organization and practice, but not a lot of thought. Learn the task – practice the task – perform the task. Thinking about the end result only slows you down.

You will go through emotional stages of frustration and doubt.

This is absolutely normal. I've met professionals in every performance domain who have flashes of doubt about their ability when faced with something new, or when faced with something they haven't done in a while. Some are frozen with fear and have to be coaxed into rehearsing or practicing. Once they get their feet under them, their confidence returns. After you establish your training process and perform a couple of times, you will gain proof that the training works.

Generally, you shouldn't have to practice more than 2 hours a day.

If you do, you haven't started training enough in advance. Learn from that mistake and don't do it again. Your training period should be long enough to do the job, but not so long that you get bored.

Take advantage of every opportunity to perform.

Beginning magicians, comedians, singers, actors, public speakers, need an audience to test their material. Some practice for thousands of hours, but they need experience in front of people in order to reset their threat radar (to teach the body that an audience is not the same as a man-eating tiger). During the process you'll make mistakes all over the place, but due to your hours and hours of training, you'll recover gracefully. You might slip, or trip, or forget a line, drop your flaming baton, but with proper training you'll be able to easily recover. Do your job and go home. You won't give a great performance every time, but sometimes a *good* performance feels great.

21. TRAINING STEPS: BY THE NUMBERS

Step 1: LOOK AT THE WHOLE PICTURE

Get an overview of your task at the beginning. You need to understand the whole puzzle in order to justify all your sacrifice. The overall picture explains why you need to run a certain way, throw a certain way, jump a certain way, stress a certain word, move to a certain mark on stage. Knowing where you have to end up explains the learning techniques you'll have to employ. Training is fairly mindless, but since we are meaning-making machines, it helps to have a clear image of the conclusion, so that we can justify working so hard. You'll learn faster, retain longer, if you understand why you're doing it and what it looks like at the end.

ABILITY
TRAINING
CONDITIONING
(*plus or minus*)
PERSONALITY
CURRENT RISKS
PERFORMANCE HISTORY
_____
ODDS OF PERFORMANCE SUCCESS

American Idol changed the entertainment business because kids now get to watch auditions on TV. Before that, entertainers seldom got to watch anyone else audition. This view of what's expected of a singer catapulted young entertainers to a new plateau. Entertainers today are much more prepared than they were years ago because the audition process doesn't surprise them. New York is now filled with brilliant young performers who are truly triple threats, ready for anything.

Step 2: REPETITION

Repetition will turn all the tiny parts of your performance into automatic behaviors. All the parts of your performance will begin to cling together into chunks of memorized behaviors, parts of your performance that happen without your thinking about them. We are built to learn this way. The more times you practice something, the more automatic it will become. When your mind wanders, automatic behavior will keep you going. Repetition may be boring, so take as many breaks as you need to maintain attention. But training 6 hours a day won't get you any further ahead than 2 hours of intense focused training. Train hard and spend the time. The training stage is boring for everyone, but making that sacrifice is what separates you from the herd. So... no whining.

Okay...maybe just a little whining.

Step 3: TRAIN SMART

Once chunks of automatic behavior start appearing you'll start to gain confidence. Begin to target the parts of the task that are not automatic yet. Train smart. Don't train more than you have to. Continue rehearsing the whole performance, but devote half of your time to the more stubborn parts. Instead of just grinding away, target your training to reduce training time and strengthen crucial parts of the task. Train smart. Eventually even the most stubborn parts of your performance will become automatic.

Step 4: ADD DISTRACTION

When horse trainers throw a saddle on a horse and the horse spooks they have to condition the horse so that it's survival alarms don't go off so easily. They'll do so by swinging bright objects within the horse's peripheral vision. The trainer waves brightly colored objects around the horse's head day after day until swinging objects no longer trigger that response. It's called desensitization. The horse's threat radar has been adjusted.

Performers in any field can desensitize themselves to distraction. This happens naturally if you perform your task regularly. If you *haven't* performed the material or the task in public yet, get used to distraction by adding it during rehearsal. It's easy and really cements the performance in your mentally and physically.

Sound that contains words is a good form of distraction. Words engage the mind more than music, making them a more formidable distraction. Music is good as long as it contains words. Vary the loudness of the sound according to your learning stage. The more secure you are, the more distraction you can add. Flashing lights, juggling, doing math problems, being struck with pillows, having wads of paper thrown at you, loud noises, cumbersome clothing, doing the task at different tempos, doing the task using different emotions, having objects swung at you...these are all forms of distraction.

If you can enlist the help of others, all the better. Add so much distraction that it actually breaks your performance. Then do it again and again until the performance holds together. Push distraction to the limit again and again until you get used to losing control - then regaining control without panicking. The distraction stage allows you to condition yourself out of panic. Like the horse, your autonomic nervous system becomes immune to the distraction because there are no painful negative results. Distraction becomes interpreted as something harmless.

When you're immune to distraction you have all the time in the world to control and shape your task.

Don't be easy on yourself. Pour on the distraction. The more distraction you can take, the more confident you can be in your performance. It tests how well you've chunked your material or skills. It's like training for battle, having bombs exploding next to you, bullets flying passed you, having to swim lagoons filled with leeches and crocodiles, and jumping out of planes. Put yourself through the wringer during training, and you will go out equipped for any performance situation. And after you successfully training this way a couple of times, you'll have confidence in the training process itself. You'll trust that, once you put yourself through the process, you'll be ready for any situation.

Step 5: SIMULATE THE SITUATION

Whenever possible, practice at the location where the performance will occur. Set up the field, the stage, or your room in the same way it will be set up at the actual performance event. The closer you can come to the actual environment, the fewer surprises you'll have later. The set up will also provide you with performance cues; things that help you remember what comes next. High divers have to practice on diving boards exactly the same length as those used at the event in order to judge their number of steps. Props can serve to remind actors of their lines. Get used to performing at the same time of day as the upcoming event. As much as possible, make the performance situation feel like home.

Step 6: RE-EVALUATE THE THREAT LEVEL

Judge the performance situation coldly. No ego. No emotion. How much distraction or stress does the situation contain? If it feels threatening, you need to add some performance aids. You can never guarantee you'll satisfy an audience. That's not your job. You're there to perform your particular task. That's it. Do your job and go home. After you've done your best, the audience will think whatever they think. You hope they like it. You hope they were impressed. Either way, it's not in your control.

Step 7: THE 4 TIME'S RULE

The training process is over when you can perform the task with added distraction, correctly 4 times in a row. Then you'll be ready for anything. If it's an extremely long task, just break the task into sections and use the 4X's rule on each section. It's not a bad thing to be bored with the task by the end of your training process. The fun arrives when you can comfortably perform any time, anywhere. Then you become the sculptor of your performance. That's when performance becomes art.

After you've graduated from the training process,

you'll need to keep the material or skill fresh. This may mean running through the task at least once a day. In fact, if the task involves memorization, it's a good idea to run through the material just before the performance too. Sometimes it helps to do it at double or triple speed. For athletes, visualize your performance just before the event. We know that mental practice has results similar to that of actual physical practice.

After Step 7, you're ready. You'll come to love this process because it will give you confidence. You'll have the knowledge that you've paid your dues and deserve to be a performer in your field. You'll be a worthy member of your performance domain.

SWIM SIDEWAYS

Sometimes it will just be impossible to give a good performance. Even if you're the most seasoned veteran, you'll sometimes encounter a situation that's distracting to concentrate. Recently, the pop singer, Beyonce' sang the National Anthem to a prerecorded vocal track. Everyone was up in arms about this, but it was actually a very smart, professional decision. She knew there would be too many distractions where she was singing. She knew the song itself contains lyrics that singers regularly miss. She didn't want to risk singing the anthem incorrectly. So...she swam sideways. She used a performance aid to make sure the performance went okay. She sang to a pre-recorded track. Smart girl!

When you know the situation will be difficult,

level the playing field. Use gimmicks. Simplify. Read your speech. Use a lead sheet with the words on it. Do a double instead of a triple. Do a layup instead of a shot from center court. Sing the note a third lower.

Don't be a victim of worry.

Simplify the task to gain control and increase confidence. That will change your whole perspective. When you're caught up in a riptide of arousal, swim sideways and make the task easier. Make things fun. Make your performance an expression of joy. That's what being a performer is truly about.

Bibliography

Aaron, S. (1986). *Stage fright: It's role in acting.* Chicago, IL: University of Chicago Press.

Al'Absi, M., Hugdahl, K., & Lovallo, W. (2002). Adrenocortical stress responses and altered working memory performance. *Psychophysiology, 39,* 95-99.

Aiello, J. R., & Douthitt, E. A. (2001). Social facilitation from Triplett to electronic performance monitoring. *Group Dynamics: Theory, Research, and Practice. 5*(3) 163-180.

Akerloff, G. A., & Shiller, R. J. (2009). *Animal spirits: How human psychology drives the economy, and why it matters for global capitalism.* Princeton, NJ: Princeton University Press.

Al'Absi, M., Bongard, S., Buchanan, T., Pincomb, G. A., Licinio, J., & Lovallo, W. R. (1997). Cardiovascular and neuroendocrine adjustment to public speaking and mental arithmetic stressors. *Psychophysiology, 34*(1997), 266-275.

Allport, F. H. (1920). The influence of the group upon association and thought. *Journal of experimental Psychology, 3*(3), 159-182.

Allport, F. H. (1924). *Social Psychology.* Boston: Houghton Miffin Company.

Allport, G. W. (1954). The historical background of modern social psychology. In G. Lindzey (Ed.), *The handbook of social psychology* (pp. 3-56). Reading, MA: Addison-Wesley.

Ambrose, S. H. (1998). Late pleistocene human population bottlenecks, volcanic winter, and differentiation of modern humans. *Journal of Human Evolution, 34*(6), 623-651. DOI: 10.1006/jhev.1998.0219.

American Psychiatric Association. (2000). *Diagnostic and statistical manual of mental Disorders* (Revised 4th ed.). Washington, DC: Author.

Apter, M.J. (2007). *Reversal Theory: The Dynamics of Motivation, Emotion and Personality* (2nd. ed.). Oxford: Oneworld Publications.

Archer, W. (1880). *Masks or faces? A study in the psychology of acting.* London: Longmans, Green and Company.

Asch, S. E. (1956). Studies of independence and conformity: A minority of one against a unanimous majority. *Psychological Monographs, 70* (Whole no. 416)

Baddeley, A. D. (2001). Is working memory still working? *American Psychologist, 56*(11), 849-864.

Baldry, H. C. (1971). *The Greek tragic theatre.* New York: W. W. Norton & Company.

Bandura, A. (1986). *Social psychology; Cognition; Social perception; Social aspects.* Englewood Cliffs, N.J.: Prentice-Hall.

Bandura, A. (1989). Regulation of cognitive processes through perceived self-efficacy. *Developmental Psychology, 25*(5), 729-735.

Barlow, D. H., & Durand, V. M. (2005). *Abnormal psychology: An integrative approach.* Belmont, CA: Thomson Wadsworth.

Baron, R. S., & Moore, D., & Sanders, G. S. (1978). Distraction as a source of drive in social facilitation research. *Journal of Personality and Social Psychology, 36,* 816-824.

Baron, R. S. (1986). Distraction-conflict theory: Progress and problems. *Advances in Experimental Social Psychology, 19,* 1-36.

Bates, J. E. (1989). Concepts and measures of temperament. In G. A Kohnstamm, J. E. Bates, & M.D. Rothbart (Eds.), *Temperament in childhood.* (pp.3-27). New York: Wiley.

Bates, B. (1991). Performance and possession: The actor and our inner demons. In G. D. Wilson (Ed.). *Psychology and performing arts.* Amsterdam: Swets & Zeitlinger.

Bayer, E. (1929). Beitrage zur Zwei komponenten theorie des Hungers [Contribution to the two component theory of hunger]. *Zeitschrift fur Psychologie, 112,* 1-54.

Beatty, M. J. (1988). Situational and predispositional correlates of public speaking anxiety. *Communication Education, 37*(1), 28-39.

Beatty, M. C., & McCroskey, J. C. (1998). Interpersonal communication as temperamental expression: A communibiological paradigm. In J. C. McCroskey, J. A. Daly, M. M. Martin, & M. J. Beatty (Eds.), *Communication and Personality: Trait perspectives.* (pp.41-67). Cresskill, NJ: Hampton Press, Inc.

Beatty, M. J., McCroskey, J. C., & Heisel, A. D. (1998). Communication apprehension as temperamental expression: A communibiological paradigm. *Communication Monographs, 64,* 197-219.

Beattie, S., Hardy, L., Savage, J., Woodman, T., Callow, N. (2011). Development and validation of a trait measure of robustness of self-confidence. *Psychology of Sport and Exercise, 12*(2), 184-191.

Beghetto, R. A. (2006) Creative self-efficacy: Correlates in middle and secondary students. *Creativity Research Journal, 18*(4), 447-457.

Beilock, S. L., Carr, T. H. (2001) On the fragility of skilled performance: What governs choking under pressure? *Journal of Experimental Psychology: General, 130,* 701-725.

Benedetti, J. (2007). *The art of the actor.* New York: Routledge.

Beilock, S. L., & Carr, T. H. (2001). On the fragility of skilled performance: What governs choking under pressure? *Journal of Experimental Psychology 130*(4), 701-725.

Benjamin, J. Ebstein, R P., Belmaker, R. H. (2002). *Molecular genetics and the human personality.* Washington, DC: American Psychiatric Publishing, Inc.

Bettleheim, B. (1976). *The uses of enchantment: The meaning and importance of fairy tales.* New York: Alfred A. Knopf.

Blascovich, J., Mendes, W. B., Hunter, S. B., & Salomon, K. (1999). Social "facilitation" as challenge and threat. *Journal of Personality and Social Psychology, 77,* 68-77.

Bond, C. F. (1982). Social facilitation: A self-presentational view. *Journal of Personality and Social Psychology, 42,* 1042-1050.

Bond, C. F., & Titus, L. J. (1983). Social facilitation: A meta analysis of 241 studies. *Psychological Bulletin, 94,* 265-292.

Bongard, S. (1995). Mental effort during active and passive coping: A dual-task analysis. *Psychophysiology, 32,* 242-248.

Borden, R. J. (1977, May). *Group size: When it matters and when it doesn't.* Paper presented at the Annual Meeting of the Midwestern Psychological Association. Chicago, Il.

Borkovec, T., Robinson, E., Pruzinsky, T., & DePree, J. A. (1983). Preliminary exploration of worry: Some characteristics and processes. *Behaviour Research and Therapy, 21*(1), 9-16.

Borkovec, T. (1994). The nature, functions and origins of worry. In G. Davey & F. Tallis (Eds.), *Worrying: Perspectives on theory, assessment and treatment* (pp. 5–34). Chichester, England: Wiley.

Bourchard, T. J. (1985). Twins reared together and apart: What they tell us about human diversity. In S. W. Fox (Ed.), *Individuality and determinism: Chemical and biological bases* (pp. 147-184). New York: Plenum Press.

Bouchard Jr., T. J. (2000). Genes, environment, and personality. In S.J. Ceci & W. M. Williams (Eds.) *The nature-nurture debate: The essential readings (Essential readings in developmental psychology.* Oxford: Wiley-Blackwell.

Bouton, M. E., Mineka, S., & Barlow, D. H. (2001). A modern learning-theory perspective on the etiology of panic disorder. *Psychological Review, 108,* 4-32.

Bovard, E. W. (1959). The effects of social stimuli on the response to stress. *Psychological Review, 66,* 267-277.

Britton D. R. , Koob, G. F., Rivier, J., & Vale, W. (1982). Intraventricular corticotropin-releasing factor enhances behavioral effects of novelty. *Life Sciences, 37,* 363-367.

Broadbent, D. E. (1958). *Perception and communication.* New York: Oxford University Press.

Broadbent D. E. (1963). Differences and interactions between stresses. *Quarterly Journal of Experimental Psychology, 15,* 205-211.

Broadbent, D. E. (1971). *Decision and Stress.* London: Academic Press.

Brown, B. R. (1968). The effects of need to maintain face on interpersonal bargaining. *Journal of Experimental Social Psychology, 4,*

107-122.

Bruner, J. S. (1986). *Actual minds, possible worlds.* Cambridge, MA: Harvard University Press.

Buckham, P. W. (1927). *Theatre of the Greeks.* Cambridge: J. Smith.

Burgoon, J. K. & Hale, J. L. (1983) A research note on the dimensions of communication reticence. *Communication Quarterly, 31*, 302-312.

Burnham, W. H. (1910). The group as a stimulus to mental activity. *Science, 31*(803), 761-767. DOI: 10.1126/science.31.803.761

Burri, C. (1931). The influence of an audience upon recall. *Journal of Educational Psychology, 22*(9), 683-690. DOI 10.1037/h0070961

Burton, D. & Naylor, S. (1997). Is anxiety really facilitative? Reaction to the myth that cognitive anxiety always impairs sport performance. *Journal of Applied Sport Psychology, 9*, 295-302.

Buss, A. H., & Plomin, R. (1975). *A temperament theory of personality development.* New York: Wiley.

Buss, A. H. (1988) *Personality: Evolutionary heritage and human distinctiveness.* Hillsdale, NJ: Erlbaum

Buss, D. M. (1991). Evolutionary personality psychology. *Annual Review of Psychology, 42*, 459-491.

Cacioppo, J. T., & Petty, R. E. (1981). Electromyographic specificity during covert information processing. *Psychophysiology, 18*, 518–523.

Caprara, G., Barbaranelli, C., Consiglio, C., Picconi, L., & Zimbardo, P. G. (2003). Personalities of politicians and voters: unique and synergistic relationships. *Journal of Personality and Social Psychology, 84*, 849–856.

Carson, S. H., Peterson, J. B., & Higgins, D. M. (2005). Reliability, validity, and factor structure of the Creative Achievement Questionnaire. *Creativity Research Journal, 17*(1), 37-50.

Caruso, C. M., Dzewaltowski, D. A., Gill, D. L., & McElroy, M. (1990). Psychological changes in competitive state anxiety during noncompetition and competitive sussess and failure. *Journal of Sport and Exercise Psychology, 12*, 6-12.

Carver, C. S. (2003). Pleasure as a sign you can attend to something else: Placing positive feelings within a general model of affect. *Cognition and Emotion, 17*(2), 241-261.

Carver, C. S., & Scheier, M. F. (1981). The self-attention-induced feedback loop and social facilitation. *Journal of Experimental Social Psychology, 17*, 545–568.

Carver, C. S. & Scheier, M. F. (1981). *Attention and Self-Regulation.* New York: Springer-Verlag.

Carver, C. S., & Scheier, M. F. (1989). A control-process perspective on anxiety. *Anxiety, Stress & Coping, 1*(1). 17-22.

Carver, C. S., & Scheier, M. F. (1998). *On self-regulation of behavior.* Cambridge: Cambridge University Press.

Carver, C. S., & White, T. 1. (1994). Behavioral inhibition, behavioral activation, and affective responses to impending reward and punishment: The BIS/BAS scales. *Journal of Personality and Social psychology, 67,* 219-333.

Cattell, R. B. (1965). *The scientific analysis of personality.* Baltimore: Penguin Books.

Chamberlain, S. T., & Hale, B. D. (2007). Competitive state anxiety and self-confidence: Intensity and direction as relative predictors of performance on a golf putting task. *Anxiety, Stress & Coping, 20*(2), 197-207.

Chapman, C. A. (1986). Boa Constrictor predation and group response in white-faced cebus monkeys. *Behaviour, 18,* 1717-172.

Charbonnier, E., Huguet, P., Brauer, M., & Monte, J. (1998). Social loafing and self-beliefs: People's collective effort depends on the extent to which they distinguished themselves as better than others. *Social Behavior and Personality, 26*(4), 329-340. doi:10.2224/sbp.1998.26.4.329

Chase, W. G., & Simon, H. A. (1973). Perception in chess. *Cognitive Psychology, 4*(1), 55-81.

Chen, S. C. (1937). Social modification of the activity of ants in nest-building. *Physiological Zoology, 10,* 420-436.

Cleckley, H. M. (1982). *The mask of sanity.* New York: Plume

Clegg, T. A. (Exec. Producer), & Attenborough, R. (Director). (1993). *Shadowlands.* [Motion Picture]. Price Entertainment in Association with Spelling Films International. 5700 Wilshire Boulevard, Los Angeles, California 90036.

Clevenger, T. (1955). A definition of stage fright. *Communication Studies, 7*(1), 26-30.

Clevenger, T. (1959). A synthesis of experimental research in stage fright. *Quarterly Journal of Speech, 45*(2), 134-145.

Clevenger, T. Jr., and King, T. R. (1961). A factor analysis of the visible symptoms of stage fright. *Speech Monographs, 28,* 245-247.

Coleridge, S. T. (1983). *Biographia literaria: or biographical sketches of my literary life and opinions.* J. Engell & W. J. Bate (Eds.), Princeton, NJ: Princeton University Press.

Costa, P. T., Jr., & McCrae, R. R. (1992). NEO-PI-R professional manual. Odessa, FL: Psychological Assessment Resources, Inc.

Cottrell, N. B. (1968). Performance in the presence of other human beings: Mere presence, audience, and affiliation effects. In E. C. Simmel, R. A. Hoppe, & G. A. Milton (Eds.), *Social facilitation and imitative behavior* (pp. 91-110). Boston: Allyn & Bacon.

Cottrell, N. B. (1972). Social facilitation. In C. G. McClintock (Ed.), *Experimental social psychology* (pp.185-236). New York: Holt, Rinehart & Winston.

Cottrell, N. B., Wack, D. L., Sekerak, G. J., & Rittle, R. H. (1968). Social facilitation of dominant responses by the presence of an audience and the mere presence of others. *Journal of Personality and Social Psychology, 9,* 245-250.

Csikszentmihalyi, M. (1990). *Flow: The psychology of optimal experience.* Harper & Row, Publishers, Inc.

Csikszentmihalyi, M., & Sawyer, R. K. (1995). Creative insight: The social dimension of a solitary moment. In R. J. Sternberg & J. E. Davidson (Eds.), *The nature of insight.* (pp.329-363). Cambridge, MA: MIT Press.

Darley, J. M., & Latane, B. (1968). Bystander intervention in emergencies: Diffusion of responsibility *Journal of Personality and Social Psychology, 8*(4), 377-383.

Darwin, C. (1899). *The expression of the emotions in man and animals.* New York: D. Appleton and Company.

Dashiell, J. F. (1930). An experimental analysis of some group effects. *The Journal of Abnormal and Social Psychology, 25(2),* 190-199.

Davidson, R. J. & Schwartz, G. E. (1976). The Psychobiology of Relaxation and Related States: A Multiprocess Theory. In D. I. Motofsky (Ed.). *Behaviour Control and Modification of Psychological Activity.* (pp. 399-442). Englewood Cliffs, NJ: Prentice Hall.

Davidson, R. J. (1995). Asymmetric brain function, affective style, and psychopathology: The role of early experience and plasticity. *Development and Psychopathology, 6,* 741–758.

Dawkins, R. (1989). The selfish gene. (2nd ed.). Oxford: Oxford University Press.

Derakshan, N., & Eysenck, M. W. (2009). Anxiety, processing efficiency, and cognitive performance: New developments from attentional control theory. *European Psychologist, 14*(2), 168-176. DOI 10.1027/1016-9040.14.2.168

Diamond, D. M., Campbell, A. M., Park, C. R., Halonen, J., & Zoladz, P. R. (2007). The temporal dynamics model of emotional memory processing: A synthesis on the neurobiological basis of stress-induced amnesia, flashbulb and traumatic memories, and the Yerkes-Dodson Law. *Neural Plasticity, 2007,* 1-33.

Diderot, D. (1883). *The paradox of acting.* W. H. Pollock (Trans.) London: Chatto & Windus, Piccadilly.

Diener, E. (1980). Deindividuation: The absence of self-awareness and self regulation in group members. In P. B. Paulus (Ed.), *Psychology of group influence* (pp. 209-242). Hillsdale, NJ: Erlbaum.

Digman, J. M. (1990). Personality structure: Emergence of the five-factor model. *Annual Review of Psychology. 41*, 417-440.

Digman, J. M. (1989). Five robust trait dimensions: Development, stability, and utility. *Journal of Personality, 57*, 195-214.

Dollinger, S. J., Urban, K. K., & James, T. A. (2004). Creativity and Openness: Further validation of two creative product measures. *Creativity research Journal, 16*(1), 35-47. DOI: 10.1207/s15326934crj16014

Doyle, J., Francis, B., & Tannenbaum, A. (1990). *Feedback control theory.* New York: Macmillan Publishing Co.

Dreyfus, H. L., & Dreyfus, S. E. (1986). *Mind over machine: The power of the human intuition and expertise in the era of the computer.* Oxford: Basil Blackwell.

Driscoll, P., Escorihuela, R. M., Fernandez-Teruel, A., Giorgi, O., Schwegler, H., Steimer, T., et al. (1998). Genetic selection and differential stress responses: The Roman lines/strains of rats. *Annals of the New York Academy of Sciences, 851*, 501-510.

Dukas, R. (2004). Causes and consequences of limited attention. *Brain Behavior and Evolution, 63*, 197-210

Dunbar, R. I. M., Cornah, L., Daly, F. J., & Bowyer, K. M. (2002). Vigilance in human groups: A test of alternative hypotheses. *Behaviour, 139*, 695-711.

Duval, S., & Wicklund, R. A. (1972). *A theory of objective self-awareness.* New York: Academic Press.

Easterbrook, J. A. (1959). The effect of emotion on cue utilization and the organization of behavior. *Psychological Review, 66*(3), 183-201.

Ebstein, R. P., Benjamin, J., & Belmaker, R. H. (2002). In R. Plomin, J. C. Defries, I. W. Craig, & P. McGuffin (Eds.), *Behavioral genetics in the postgenomic era.* Washington DC: American Psychological Association.

Egan, S., & Stelmack, R. M. (2003). A personality profile of Mount Everest climbers. *Personality and Individual Differences*, 34(8), 1491-1494. DOI: 10.1016/S0191-8869(02)00130-7

Enright, P. (2007, September 12). Pulling back the curtain on stage fright. *Msnbc.com.* Retrieved May 25, 2011, from http://www.msnbc.msn.com/id/20631646/ns/health-mental_health/t/pulling-back-curtain-stage-fright/

Epstein, S. (1972). Comments on Dr. Cattell's paper. In C. D. Spielberger's (Ed.) *Anxiety: Current trends and research.* New York: Academic Press.

Ericsson, K. A. (1988). Analysis of memory performance in terms of memory skill. In R. J. Sternberg (Ed.) *Advances in the Psychology of Human Intelligence. Vol. 4.* Hillsday, NJ: Lawrence Erlbaum

Associates, Inc.

Ericsson, K. A., & Charness, N. (1994). Expert performance: Its structure and acquisition. *American Psychologist, 49*(8), 725-747.

Ericsson, K. A., & Kintsch, W. (1995). Long-Term working memory. *Psychological Review, 102*(2), 211-245.

Eysenck, H. J. (1967). *The biological basis of personality.* Springfield, IL: Charles C. Thomas.

Eysenck, M.V., & Calvo, M. (1992). Anxiety and performance: The processing efficiency theory. *Cognition and Emotion, 6,* 409-434.

Eysenck, H. J., & Eysenck, S. B. G. (1975). *Manual of the Eysenck personality questionnaire.* London: Hodder and Stoughton.

Eysenck, H. J., & Eysenck, M. W. (1985). *Personality and individual differences: A natural science approach.* New York: Plenum Press.

Eysenck, H. J. (1990). Biological dimensions of personality. In L. A. Pervin (Ed.), *Handbook of personality: Theory and research* (pp. 244-276). New York: Guilford.

Eysenck, H. J. (1990a). Genetic and environmental contributions to individual differences: The three major dimensions of personality. *Journal of Personality, 58*, 245-261.

Eysenck, H. J. (1990b). Biological dimensions of personality. In L. A. Pervin (Ed.) *Handbook of personality: Theory and research.* (244-276). New York: Guilford Press.

Eysenck, H. J. (1992). A reply to Costa and McCrae. P or A and C: The role of theory. *Personality and Individual Differences, 13*, 867–868.

Eysenck, H. J. (1997). Personality and experimental psychology: The unification of psychology and the possibility of a paradigm. *Journal of Personality and Social Psychology, 73*, 1224-1237.

Eysenck, H. J., Barrett, P., Wilson, G., & Jackson, C. (1992). Primary trait measurement of the 21 components of the PEN system. *European Journal of Psychological Assessment, 8,*   109–117.

Eysenck, M. W., Santos, R., Derakshan, N., & Calvo, M. G. (2007). Anxiety and cognitive performance: Attentional control theory. Emotion, 7(2) 336-353.

Ericsson, K. A. & Charness, N. (1994). Expert performance: Its structure and acquisition. *American Psychology, 49*(8), 725-747.

Ericsson, K. A., & Kintsch, W. (1995). Long-term working memory. *Psychological Review, 102*, 211-245.

Farnsworth, P. R. (1928). Concerning so-called group effects. *Journal of Genetic Psychology, 35,* 587-594.

Forgas, J. P., Brennan, G., Howe, S., Kane, F. J., & Sweet, S. (1980). Audience effects on squash players' performance. *The Journal of Social Psychology, 111,* 41–47.

Festinger, L. (1957). *A theory of cognitive dissonance*. Stanford, CA: Stanford University.

Fredrikson, M., & Gunnarsson, R. (1992). Psychobiology of stage fright: The effect of public performance on neuroendocrine, cardiovascular and subjective reaction. *Biological Psychology, 33*(1), 52-62. DOI: 10.1016/0301-511(92)90005-5

Freedman, J. L., Birsky, J., & Cavoukian, A. (1980). Environmental determinants of behavioral contagion: *Density and number. Basic and Applied Social Psychology, 1*(2), 155-161. DOI: 10.1207/s15324834basp0102_4

Fishbein, M. (1963). An investigation of the relationships between beliefs about an object and the attitude toward that object. *Human Relations, 16*(3), 233-239.

Gates, G. S. (1924). The effect of an audience upon performance. *Journal of Abnormal Psychology and Social Psychology, 18*(4), 334-342.

Gates, M. F., & Allee, W. C. (1933). Conditioned behavior of isolated and grouped cockroaches in a simple maze. *Journal of Comparative Psychology, 2,* 331-358. Geen, R. G. (1976). Test anxiety, observation, and range of cue utilization. British Journal of Social and Clinical Psychology, 15(3), 253-259.

Geen, R. G. (1979). Effects of being observed on learning following success and failure. *Motivation and Emotion, 3,* 355-371. DOI: 10.1007/BF00994050

Geen, R. G. (1991). Social motivation. *Annual Review of Psychology, 42,* 377-399.

Gill, D. L. (1994). A sport and exercise psychology perspective on stress. *Quest, 46,* 20-27. *8*(4), 288-296.

Gilkinson, H. (1942). Social fears as reported by students in college speech classes. *Speech Monographs, 9,* 141-160.

Glasser, W. (1986). *Control theory in the classroom.* New York: HarperCollins Publishers Inc.

Glazer, S. R. (1981). Oral communication apprehension and avoidance: The current status of treatment research. *Communication Education, 30,* 321-341.

Gleik, J. (1987). *Chaos: Making a new science.* New York: Penguin Group.

Goffman, E. (1955). On facework. *Psychiatry, 18,* 213- 231.

Goffman, E. (1959). *The presentation of self in everyday life.* New York: Doubleday-Anchor.

Goldberg, L. R. (1990). An alternative "description of personality": The Big-Five factor structure. *Journal of Personality and Social Psychology, 59*(6), 1216-1229.

Goldberg, L. R. (1992). The development of markers for the Big-

Five factor structure. *Psychological Assessment, 4*, 26–42.

Goldberg, L. R., Johnson, J. A., Eber, H. W., Hogan, R. Ashton, M. C., Cloninger, C. R., & Gough, H. G. (2006). The international personality item pool and the future of public-domain personality measures. *Journal of Research in Personality, 40*(1), 84-96. Proceedings of the 2005 Meeting of the Association of Research in Personality. DOI:10.1016/j.jrp.2005.08.007

Goldstein, K., & Scheerer, M. (1941). Abstract and concrete behavior. *Psychological Monographs, 53*, 110-130.

Goldstein, T. R., Wu, K. & Winner, E. (2009-2010). Actors are skilled in theory of mind but not in empathy. *Imagination, Cognition and Personality, 29*(2), 115-133.

Goode, M. I. (2003). *Stage fright in music performance and its relationship to the unconscious.* Oak Park, IL: Trumpetworks Press.

Goodman, J. (1995). First Knight of the Stage." *Contemporary Review 266*, 310-312.

Gould, D., Weiss, M., & Weinberg, R. S. (1981). Psychological characteristics of successful and non-successful Big Ten wrestlers. *Journal of Sport Psychology, 31*(1), 69-81.

Gould, D., Tuffey, S. (1996). Zones of optimal functioning research: A review and critique. *Anxiety, Stress, and Coping, 9*, 53-68.

Grant, T., & Dajee, K. (2002). Types of audience, types of actor: Interactions of mere presence and personality type in a simple mathematical task. *Personality and Individual Differences, 35*, 633-639.

Gray, J. A. (1981). A critique of Eysenck's theory of personality. In H. J. Eysenck (Ed). *A model for personality.* (pp. 246–276). New York: Springer.

Gray, J. A. (1982). *The neuropsychology of anxiety.* Oxford: Clarendon.

Gray, J. A. (1991). The neuropsychology of temperament. In J. Strelau & A. Angleitner (Eds.) *Explorations in temperament: International perspectives on theory and measurement. perspectives on individual differences* (pp. 105-128), New York: Plenum Press.

Gray, J. A. & McNaughton, N. (1996). The neuropsychology of anxiety: Reprise. In D. A. Hope (Ed.) *Perspectives on anxiety, panic and fear* (The 43rd Annual Nebraska Symposium on Motivation) pp. 61-134). Linclon: Nebraska University Press.

Gray, J.A., & McNaughton, N. (2000). *The Neuropsychology of anxiety: an enquiry into the functions of the septo-hippocampal system.* Oxford: Oxford University Press.

Green, D. (2002). *Performance success: Performing your best under pressure.* New York: Routledge.

Griffin, M. (2001). The phenomenology of the alone condition:

More evidence for the role of aloneness in social facilitation. *Journal of Psychology, 135*(1), 125-127.

Guerin, B. (1983). Social facilitation and social monitoring: a test of three models. *British Journal of Social Psychology, 22*, 203–214.

Guerin, B. (1986). Mere presence effects in humans: A review. *Journal of Experimental Social Psychology, 22*, 38-77.

Guerin, B. (1993). *Social facilitation.* Cambridge, England: Cambridge University Press.

Guerin, B., & Innes, J. M. (1982). Social facilitation and social monitoring: A new look at Zajonc's mere presence hypothesis. *British Journal of Social Psychology, 21*, 7-18.

Haines, H., & Vaughan, V. M. (1979). Was 1898 a "great date" in the history of experimental social psychology? *Journal of the History of the Behavioral Sciences, 15*(4), 323-332. DOI: 10.1002/1520-6696(197910)15:4<323::AID-JHBS2300150405>3.0.CO;2-I

Hamilton W.D. (1971). Geometry for the selfish herd. *Journal of Theoretical Biology. 31*, 295-311.

Hammond, J., & Edelmann, R. J. (1991). The act of being: personality characteristics of professional actors, amateur actors, and non-actors. In G. D. Wilson (Ed.), *Psychology and performing arts* (pp. 123–131). Amsterdam: Swets & Zeitlinger.

Handford, C., Davids, K., Bennett, S., & Button, C. (1997). Skill acquisition in sport: Some applications of an evolving practice ecology. *Journal of Sports Sciences, 15*, 621-640.

Haney, C., Banks, C. & Zimbardo, P. G., (1973). Interpersonal dynamics in a simulated prison. *International Journal of Criminology and Penology, 1*, 69-97.

Hanin, Y. L. (1995). Individual zones of optimal functioning (IZOF) model: An idiographic approach to performance anxiety. In K. Henschlen & W. Straub (Eds.) *Sport psychology: An analysis of athlete behavior* (pp. 103-119). Longmeadow, MA: Movement Publications.

Hanton, S., Mellalieu, S. D., & Hall, R. (2004). Self-confidence and anxiety interpretation: A qualitative investigation. *Psychology of Sport & Exercise, 5*, 477-495.

Hardy, L. (1990). A catastrophe model of anxiety and performance. In J. G. Jones & L. Hardy (Eds.), *Stress and Performance in Sport* (pp. 81–106). Chichester: Wiley.

Hardy, L. (1996b). A test of catastrophe models of anxiety and sports performance against multidimensional theory models using the method of dynamic differences. *Anxiety, Stress and Coping: An International Journal, 9*, 69–86.

Hardy, L. (1996a). Testing the predictions of the cusp catastrophe model of anxiety and   performance. *The Sport Psychologist, 10*, 140–156.

Hardy, L. (1999). Stress, anxiety and performance. *Journal of Science and Medicine in Sport, 2*(3), 227-233.

Hardy, L., Beattie, S., & Woodman, T. (2007). Anxiety-induced performance catastrophes: Investigating effort required as an asymmetry factor. *British Journal of Psychology, 98*(1), 15-31.

Hardy, L., & Fazey, J. (1987, June). *The inverted-U hypothesis: A catastrophe for sport psychology.* Paper presented at the meeting of the North American Society for the Psychology of Sport and Physical Activity, Vancouver, British Columbia.

Hardy, L. & Hutchinson, A. (2007). Effects of performance anxiety on effort and performance in rock climbing: A test of processing efficiency theory. *Anxiety, Stress & Coping, 20*(2), 147-161.

Hare, R. D. (1993). Without Conscience: The disturbing world of the psychopaths among us. New York: Simon & Schuster

Harlow, H. F. (1932) Social facilitation of feeding in the albino rat. *Journal of Genetic Psychology, 41*, 211-221.

Hayward, P. (2002). *Leisure and tourism.* Portsmouth, NH: Heinemann Educational Books.

Hebb, D. O. (1949). *Organization of behavior.* New York: Wiley.

Hebb, D. O. (1955). Drives and the C.N.S. (conceptual nervous system). *Psychological Review, 62*(4), 243–254.

Hebb, D. O. (1976). Physiological learning theory. *Journal of Abnormal Child Psychology, 44*(4), 309-314.

Henchy, T., & Glass, D. C. (1968). Evaluation apprehension and the social facilitation of dominant and subordinate responses. *Journal of Personality and Social Psychology, 10*(4), 446-454.

Heider, F., Simmel, M. (1944). An Experimental Study of Apparent Behavior. *American Journal of Psychology, 57*(2), 243-259.

Heider, F. (1958). *The psychology of interpersonal relations.* New York: Wiley.

Highlen, P.S., & Bennett, B.B. (1979). Psychological characteristics of successful and nonsuccessful elite wrestlers: an exploratory study. *Journal of Sport Psychology, 1*, 123–137.

Hollingworth, H. (1935). *The psychology of the audience.* New York: American Book Company.

Holroyd, M. (2009). *A strange eventful history: The dramatic lives of Ellen Terry, Henry Irving, and their remarkable families.* New York: Farrar, Strauss, and Giroux.

Horace. (2001). Ars poetica. D. A. Russell (Trans.). In V. B. Leitch, W. E. Cain, L. A. Finke, V. Finke, B. E. Johnson, J. McGowan, J. J. Williams, (Eds.), *The Norton Anthology of Theory and Criticism*. New York: Norton, (pp. 124-135).

Horvath, C. W. (1995). Biological origins of communicator style. *Communication Quarterly, 43*(4), 394-429.

Huguet, P., Galvaing, M. P., Monteil, J. M., & Dumas, F. (1999). Social presence effects in the Stroop task: Further evidence for an attentional view of social facilitation. *Journal of Social and Personality Psychology, 77,* 1011–1025.

Hull, C. L. (1943). *Principles of Behavior: An Introduction to Behavior Theory.* New York: Appleton-Century-Crofts.

Innes, J. M., & Young, R. F. (1975). The effect of presence of an audience, evaluation apprehension and objective self-awareness on learning. *Journal of Experimental Social Psychology, 11,* 35–42.

Innes, J. M., & Gordon, M. I. (1985). The effect of mere presence and a mirror on performance of a motor task. *The Journal of Social Psychology, 125,* 479–484.

Iso-Aloha, S. E., & Hatfield, B. (1985). *Psychology of sports.* Dubuque, IA: Brown.

Iso-Ahola SE, Hatfield B. (1986). Psychological characteristics and pain tolerance of successful athletes. In Iso-Ahola SE, Hatfield B (Eds.), *Psychology of Sports.* pp. 151-176. Dubuque, IA: William C. Brown.

Jackson, J. M., & Latané, B. (1981). All alone in front of all those people: Stagefright as a function of number and type of co-performers and audience. *Journal of Personality and Social Psychology, 40*(1), 73-85.

Jackson, J. M., & Williams, K. D. (1985). Social loafing on difficult tasks: Working collectively can improve performance. *Journal of Personality and Social Psychology, 49,* 937-942.

Jahoda, G. (2007). *A history of social psychology: From the eighteenth-century Enlightenment to the Second World War.* Cambridge, MA: Cambridge University Press.

Jones, E. E., & Gerard, H. B. (1967). *Fundamentals of social psychology.* New York: John Wiley and Sons, Inc.

Jones, J. G. (1991). Recent developments and current issures in competitive state anxiety
research. *The Sports Psychologist, 4,* 152-155.

Jones, G., Hanton, S., & Swain, A. (1994). Intensity and direction as dimensions of competitive symptoms in elite and non-elite sports performers. *Personality and Individual Differences, 17,* 657-663.

Jones, G., & Swain, A. (1992). Intensity and direction as dimensions of competitive state anxiety and relationships with competitiveness. *Perceptual and Motor Skills, 74,* 467-472.

Jones, G., & Swain, A. (1995). Predispostions to experience debilitative and facilitative anxiety in elite and non-elite performers. *The Sport Psychologist, 9,* 201-211.

Jung, C. G. (1970). *The structure and dynamics of the psyche* (collected works of C. G. Jung, (Volume 8). G. Adler & R. F. C. Hull (Trans.). Princeton, NJ: Princeton University Press.

Kaufman, B. E. (1999). Emotional arousal as a source of bounded rationality. *Journal of Economic Behavior & Organization, 38*(2), 135-144.

Kaufman, J. C., & Beghetto, R. A. (2009) Beyond the big and little: The four c model of creativity. *Review of General Psychology, 13*(1), 1-12.

Kelly, G. A. (1955). *The psychology of personal constructs*. New York: Norton.

Kelly, L., & Keaten, J. A. (2000). Treating communication anxiety: Implications of the communibiological paradigm.

Kent, J. A. (Ed.), (2007). *Kent and Riegel's handbook of industrial chemistry and biotechnology*. (vol. 1). New York: Springer Science and Business Media, LLC.

Keogh, E., & French, C. C. (2001). Test anxiety, evaluative stress, and susceptibility to distraction from threat. *European Journal of Personality, 15,* 123–141.

Kessler, R. C., McGonagle, K. A., Zhao, s., Nelson, C. B., Hughes, M., Eshleman, S., Wittchen, H. U., & Kendler, K. S. (1994). Lifetime and 12-month prevalence of DSM-III-R psychiatric disorders among persons aged 15-54 in the United States: Results from the national comorbidity survey. *Archives of General Psychiatry, 51*(1), 8-19.

Kiehl, K. A., Smith, A. M., Hare, R. D., Mendrek, A., Forster, B. B., Brink, J., & Liddle, P. F. (2001). Limbic abnormalities in affective processing by criminal psychopaths as revealed by functional magnetic resonance imaging. *Biological Psychiatry*, 50, 677-684.

Kiesler, S. B. (1966). Stress, affiliation, and performance. *Journal of Experimental Social Psychology, 1,* 227-235.

Knowles, E. S. (1983). Social physics and the effects of others: Tests of the effects of audience size and distance on social judgments and behavior. *Journal of Personality and Social Psychology, 45*(6), 1263-1279.

Krane, V., & Williams, J. (1987). Performance and somatic anxiety, cognitive anxiety, and confidence changes prior to competition. *Journal of Sport Behavior*, 10, 47-56.

Krane, V., Joyce, D., & Rafeld, J. (1994). Competitive anxiety, situation criticality, and softball performance. *The Sport Psychologist, 8,* 58-72.

Kumar, S., Soren, S., Chaudrey, S. (2009). Hallucinations: Etiology ad clinical implications. Industrial Psychiatry Journal, 18(2), 119-126.

Lachter, J., Forster, K. I., Ruthruff, E. (2004). Forty-five years after Broadbent (1958): Still no identification without attention. *Psychological Review, 111*(4), 880-913.

Landers, D. M. (1980). The arousal-performance relationship revisited. *Research Quarterly for Exercise and Sport, 51*, 77-90.

Lane, A., Sewell, D. F., Terry, P., Bartram, D., Nesti, M. S. (1999). Confirmatory factor analysis of the Competitive Stage Anxiety Inventory-2. *Journal of Sports Sciences, 17*(6), 505-512. DOI: 10.1080/026404199365812

Latane', B. & Darley, J. M. (1968). Group inhibition of bystander intervention in emergencies. Journal of Personality and Social Pychology, 10(3), 215-221.

Latane, B., Williams, K. D., & Harkins, S. G. (1979). Many hands make light the work: the causes and consequences of social loafing. *Journal of Personality and Social Psychology, 37*, 822–832.

Lazarus, R.S. (1990). Constructs of the mind in adaptation. In N. L. Stein, B. Leventhal, & T. Trabasso (Eds.), *Psychological and Biological Approaches to Emotion*, (pp. 3-19). Hillsdale, New Jersey: Lawrence Erlbaum, Associates.

Lazarus. R. (1991*). Emotion and adaptation.* New York: Oxford University Press.

Lazarus, R. S. (1993). Why we should think of stress as a subset of emotion. In L. Goldberger & S. Breznitz (Eds.) *Handbook of Stress: theoretical and clinical aspects,* (pp. 234-257). New York, N.Y: Free Press.

Leary, M. R., & Kowalski, R. M. (1995). *Social anxiety.* New York: Guilford Press.

LeDoux, J. E. (1996). *The emotional brain: The mysterious underpinnings of emotional life.* New York: Simon & Schuster.

Levav, J., & Fitzsimons, G. J. (2006). When questions change behavior: The role of ease of representation. Psychological Science, 17, 207-213. DOI: 10.1111/j.1467-9280.2006.01687.x

Levenson, H. (1981). Differentiating among internality, powerful others, and chance. In H. M. Lefcourt (Ed.), *Research with the locus of control construct* (Vol. 1, pp. 15-63). New York: Academic Press.

Lewin, K. (1936). *Principles of topological psychology.* New York: McGraw-Hill, Inc.

Liddell, H. (1950). The role of vigilance in the development of animal neurosis. In P. H. Hoch & J. Zubin, (Eds.) *Anxiety* (pp. 183-196). New York: Grune & Stratton.

Lockwood, A. H. (1989). Medical problems of musicians. *New England Journal of Medicine, 320*, 221-227.

Lucas, R., & Fujita, F. (2000). Factors influencing the relation between extraversion and pleasant affect. *Journal of Personality and Social Psychology, 79,* 1039-1056.

Lupien, S. J., Maheu, F., Tu, M., Fiocco, A., & Schramek, T. E. (1997). The effects of stress and hormones on human cognition: Implications for the field of brain and cognition. *Brain and Cognition, 65*(3), 209-237. doi:10.1016/j.bandc.2007.02.007

Luria, A. R. (1961). *The role of speech in the regulation of normal and abnormal behavior.* Oxford: Pergamon Press.

Luszczynska, A., Gutierrez-Dona, B., & Schwarzer, R. (2005). General self-efficacy in various domains of human functioning: Evidence from five countries. *International Journal of Psychology, 30*(2), 80-89.

MacLeod, C. (1990). Mood disorders and cognition. In M. W. Eysenck (Ed.), *Cognitive Psychology: An International Review* (pp. 9-56). Chichester: Wiley.

Manstead, A. S. R., & Semin, G. R. (1980). Social facilitation effects: Mere enhancement of dominant responses? *British Journal of Social and Clinical Psychology, 19,* 119–136.

Marchant-Haycox, S. E., & Wilson, G. D. (1992). Personality and stress in performing artists. *Personality and Individual Differences, 13,* 1061–1068.

Martens, R. (1968). *Effects of an audience on learning and performance of a complex motor skill.* Unpublished doctoral dissertation, University of Illinois at Urbana-Champaign.

Martens, R., & Landers, D. M. (1970). Motor performance under stress. Journal of Personality and Social Psychology, 16(1), 29-37.

Martens, R. (1969). Effect of an audience on learning and performance of a complex motor skill. *Journal of Personality and Social Psychology, 12,* 252–260.

Martens, R. (1971). Anxiety and motor behavior: A review. *Journal of Motivational Behavior, 3*(2), 151-179.

Martens, R. (Ed.) (1977). *Sport Competition Anxiety Test.* Champaign, Il: Human Kinetics.

Martens, R., Burton, D., Vealey, R. S., Bump, L. A. & Smith, D. E. (1990). Competitive state anxiety inventory-2. In R. Martens, R. Vealey & D. Burton (Eds.), *Competitive Anxiety.* (pp.193-208). Champaign, IL: Human Kinetics.

Martens, R. & Landers, D. M. (1972). Evaluation potential as a determinant of coaction effects. *Journal of Experimental Social Psychology, 8*(4), 347-359. DOI: 10.1016/0022-1031(72)90024-8

Martens, R., Vealey, R. S., & Burton, D. (1990). *Competitive anxiety in sport.* Champaign, IL: Human Kinetics Publishers, Inc.

Martin, B. (1961). The assessment of anxiety by physiological behavioral measures.

Psychological Bulletin, 58, 234-255.

Martin, M. (1983). Cognitive failure: Everyday and laboratory performance. *Bulletin of the Psychonomic Society, 21*(2), 97-100. Martin, J. J., & Cutler, K. (2002). An exploration study of flow and motivation in theater actors. *Journal of Applied Sport Psychology 14*(4), 344-352.

Martin, N., & Jardine, R. (1986). Eysenck's contributions to behaviour genetics. In S. Modgill & I. Modgill (Eds.), *Hans Eysenck: Consensus and controversy* (pp. 13-47). London: Falmer.

Mathews, A. (1990). Why worry? The cognitive function of anxiety. *Behaviour Research and Therapy,* 28(6), 455-468. doi:10.1016/0005-7967(90)90132-3

Maxwell, J. C. (1868). On governors. *Proceedings of the Royal Society of London, 16,* 270-283.

May, R. (1970). Psychotherapy and the daimonic. In J. Campbell (Ed.) *Myth, Dreams and Religion.* (pp. 196-210). New York: Dutton. New York: MJF Books.

May, R. (1996). *The meaning of anxiety.* New York: W. W. Norton Company, Inc.

McCrae, R. R., & Costa, P. T. Jr. (1985). Comparison of IPI and psychoticism scales with measure of the five-factor model of personality. *Personality and Individual Differences, 6*(5), 587-597.

McCrae, R. R., & Costa, P. T. Jr. (1987). Validation of the five-factor model of personality across instruments and observers. *Journal of Personality and Social Psychology, 52,* 81-90.

McCrae, R. R., Costa, P. T. (1990). *Personality in adulthood.* New York: Guilford.

McCrae, R. R., & Costa, P. T. Jr. (1997). Personality and trait structure as a human universal. *American Psychologist, 52,* 509-516.

McCroskey, J. C., Richmond, V. P., Heisel, A. D., & Hayhurst, J. L. (2004). Eysenck's BIG THREE and communication traits: Communication traits as manifestations of temperament. *Communication Research Reports, 21,* 404-410.

McCroskey, J.C. (1977). Oral communication apprehension: A summary of recent theory and research. *Human Communication Research, 4,* 78-96.

McCroskey, J. C., Beatty, M. J., Kearney, P., & Plax, T. G. (1985). *Communication Quarterly, 33*(3), 165-173.

McCroskey, J. C., Heisel, A. D., & Richmond, V. P. (2001). Eysenck's big three and communication traits: Three correlational studies. Communication Monographs, 68, 360-366.

Mellalieu, S. D., Hanton, S., & Jones, G. (2003). Emotional labeling and competitive anxiety in preparation and competitition. *The Sport Psychologist, 17,* 157-174.

Mertler, C. A., & Vannatta, R. A. (2005). Advanced and multivariate statistical methods. Glendale, CA: Pyrczak Publishing.

Meumann, E. (1904). Haus und Schularbeit: Experimente an kindern der Volkschul [Home and schoolwork: Experiments on children in school]. *Die Deutsche Schule, 8,* 278-431.

Mezzich, J. E., Kleinman, A., Fabrega, H., Jr., Good, B., Johnson-Powel, G., Lin, K. M., Manson, S., & Parron, D. (1992). *Cultural proposals for DSM-IV.* Submitted to the DSM-IV Task Force by the Steering Committee, NIMH-Sponsored Group on Culture and Diagnosis.

Milgram, S. (1963). Behavioral study of obedience. *The Journal of Abnormal and Social Psychology, 67*(4), 371-378.

Milgram, S. (1965). Liberating effects of group pressure. *Journal of Personality and Social Psychology, 1*(2), 127-134.

Miller, G. (1956). The magical number seven, plus or minus two: some limits on our capacity for processing information. *Psychological Review, 63(2), 81-97.*

Mischel, W., & Shoda, Y. (1995). A cognirive-affective system theory of personality: Reconceptualizing situations, dispositions, dynamics, and invariance in personality structure. *Psychological Review, 102*(2), 246-268.

Modigliani, A. (1971). Embarrassment, facework, and eye contact: Testing a theory of embarrassment. *Journal of Personality and Social Psychology, 17*(1), 15-24.

Morris, L. W. Davis, M. A., & Hutchings, C. H. (1981). Cognitive and emotional components of anxiety: Literature review and a revised Worry-Emotionality Scale. *Journal of Educational Psychology, 73*, 541-555.

Morrison, J. (2006). *DSM-IV Made Easy: The clinicians guide to diagnosis.* New York: Guilford Press.

Mullen, R., & Hardy, L. (2000). State anxiety and motor performance: testing the conscious processing hypothesis. *Journal of Sports Sciences, 18*(10), 785-799.

Mwmacis (2008, June 13). This is not Leslie Uggams June is Bustin Out All Over [Video file] Retrieved from http://www.youtube.com/watch?v=Mrma76T5Wa4

Nagel, J., Himle, D., & Papsdorf, J. (1981). Coping with performance anxiety. *NATS Bulletin, 37*, 26-33.

Narayanan, L., Menon, S., & Levine, E. L. (1995). Personality structure: A culture-specific examination of the five-factor model. *Journal of Personality Assessment 64*, 51-62.

Nettle, D. (2006). Psychological profiles of professional actors. *Personality and Individual Differences, 40*, 375-383.

Nettle, D. (2007). Empathizing and systemizing: What are they, and what do they contribute to our understanding of psychological sex differences? *British Journal of Psychology 98*, 237-255.

Neuliep, J. W., Chadouir, M., & McCroskey, J. C. (2003). A cross-cultural test of the association between temperament and communication apprehension. *Communication Research Reports, 20*(4), 320-330.

Noice, T., & Noice, H. (1997). *The nature of expertise in professional acting.* Mahwah, NJ: Lawrence Erlbaum Associates, Publishers.

Nolen-Hoeksema, S., Wisco, B. E., and Lyubomirsky, S. (2008). Rethinking rumination. *Perspectives on Psychological Science, 3*(5), 400-424.

Olivier, L. (1982). *Confessions of an actor.* New York: Simon and Schuster.

Parfitt, G., & Hardy, L. (1987). Further evidence for the differential effects of competitive state anxiety upon a number of cognitive and motor subsystems. *Journal of Sports Sciences, 5*, 62-63.

Park, C. R., Campbell, A. M., Woodson, J. C., Smith, T. P., Fleshner, M., & Diamond, D. M. (2006). Permissive influence of stress in the expression of a U-shaped relationship
between serum corticosterone levels and spatial memory errors in rats. *Dose-Response, 4,* 55-74.

Paulus, P. B., & Murdoch, P. (1971). Anticipated evaluation and audience presence in the enhancement of dominant responses. *Journal of Experimental Social Psychology, 7,* 280-291.

Pedersen, N. l., Plomin, R., McClearn, G. E., & Friberg, L. (1988). Neuroticism, extraversion, and related traits in adult twins reared apart and reared together. *Journal of Personality and Social Psychology, 55*, 950-957.

Pessin, J. (1933). The comparative effects of social and mechanical stimulation on memorizing. *American Journal of Psychology, 45.* 263-270.

Pessin, J., & Husband, R. W. (1933). Effects of social stimulation on human maze learning. *Journal of Abnormal and Social Psychology, 25,* 148-154.

Plaze, M., Bartres-Faz, D., Martinot, J., Januel, D., Bellivier, F., De Beaurepaire, R., Chanraud, S., Andoh, J., Lefaucheur, J., Artiges, E., Pallier, C., Paillere-Martinot, M. (2006). Left superior temporal gyrus activation during sentence perception negatively correlates with auditory hallucination severity in schizophrenia patients. *Schizophrenia Research, 87*(1-3), 1-7

Puchner, M. (2002). *Stage fright: Modernism, anti-theatricality, and drama.* Baltimore, MD: Johns Hopkins University Press.

Rammstedt, B., & John, O. P. (2007). Measuring personality in one minute or less: A 10-item short version of the Big Five Inventory in English and German. *Journal of Research in Personality, 4,* 203-212.

Rattenborg, N. C., Lima, S. L., & Amlaner, C. J. (1999). Half-awake to the risk of predation. *Nature, 397,* 397-398. doi:10.1038/17037

Richmond, V.P., & McCroskey, J.C (1979). Management communication style, tolerance for disagreement and innovativeness as predictors of employee satisfaction: A comparison of single-factor, two-factor, and multiple-factor approaches. In D. Nimmo (Ed.), *Communication Yearbook, 3,* New Brunswick, N.J: Transaction.

Rodrigues, A., & Levine, R. V. (Eds.). (1999). *Reflections on 100 years of experimental social psychology.* New York: Basic Books.

Rose, L. M., & Fedigan, L. M. (1995). Vigilance in white-faced capucins, Cebus capucinus, in Costa Rica. *Animal Behavior, 49,* 63-70.

Sanders, G.S. (1981). Driven by distraction: An integrative review of social facilitation theory and research. *Journal of Experimental Social Psychology, 17*(3), 227-251. DOI:10.1016/0022-1031(81)90024-X

Sanna, L. J. (1992). Self-efficacy theory: Implications for social facilitation and social loafing. *Journal of Personality and Social Psychology, 62,* 774-786.

Sapolsky, R. M. (1990). Stress in the wild. *Scientific American, 262,* 116-123.

Sapolsky, R. M. (2000) *A primate's memoir.* New York: Simon & Schuster.

Sawyer, R. K. (2005). Acting. In J. C. Kaufman (Ed.), *Creativity across domains: Faces of the Muse.* (pp. 41-57). Mahwah, NJ: Lawrence Erlbaum Associates.

Sawyer, R. K. (2010, October 28). Group genius and collective intelligence. Retrieved from Creativity and Innovation http://keithsawyer.wordpress.com/2010/10/28/group-genius-and-collective-intelligence/

Saucier, G. (1994). Mini-markers: A brief version of Golberg's unipolar Big-Five markers. *Journal of Personality Assessment, 63,* 506-516.

Schachter, S. & Singer, J. E. (1962). Cognitive, Social, and Physiological Determinants of Emotional State. *Psychological Review, 69*(5), 379-399.

Scheier, M. F., Carver, C. S., & Bridges, M. W. (1994). Distinguishing optimism from neuroticism (and trait anxiety, self-mastery, and self-esteem): A reevaluation of the life orientation test. *Journal of Personality and Social Psychology, 67*, 1063-1078.

Scheier, M. F., Matthews, K. A., Owens, J. F., Schulz, R., Bridges, M. W., Magovern, G. J., Sr., & Carver, C. S. (1999). Optimism and rehospitalization following coronary artery bypass graft surgery. *Archives of Internal Medicine,159*, 829-835.

Schlosberg, H. (1954). Three dimensions of emotion. *Psychological Review, 61*(2), 81–88.

Sengupta, N N., & Sinha, C. P N. (1926). Mental work in isolation and in group*Indian Journal of Psychology, 1*, 106-110.

Seta, C. E., & Seta, J. J. (1983). The impact of personal equity processes on performance in a group setting. In P. B. Paulus (Ed.), *Basic group processes* (pp. 121-143). New York: Springer-Verlag.

Seta, C. E., & Seta, J. J. (1995). When audience presence is enjoyable: The influences of audience awareness of prior success on performance and task interest. *Basic and Applied Social Psychology, 16*(1-2), 95-108.

Shakespeare, W. (1914) Hamlet, Prince of Denmark. (Craig, W.J., Ed.) London: The Oxford Shakespeare.

Sherer, M., Maddux, J. E., Mercandante, B., Prentice-Dunn, S., Jacobs, B., & Rogers, R. W. (1982). The Self-Efficacy Scale: Construction and validation. *Psychological Reports, 51*, 663-671.

Shiffrin, R. M., & Schneider, W. (1977). Controlled and automatic human information processing. II: perceptual learning, automatic attending, and a general theory. *Psychological Review, 84*, 127–190.

Slaughter, W. S. (2002). *The Linearized Theory of Elasticity*. Boston: Birkhauser.

Smallwood, J., & Schooler, J. W. (2006). The restless mind. *Psychological Bulletin, 132*(6), 946-958.

Snyder, M. (1987). *Public appearances, private realities: the psychology of self-monitoring*. New York: W. H. Freeman Company.

Spence, K. W. (1956). *Behavior Theory and Conditioning*. New Haven: Yale University Press.

Spence, K. W. (1958). A theory of emotionally based drive (D) and its relation to performance in simple learning situations. *American Psychologist, 13*:131-41.

Spielberger, C. D. (1966). Theory and research on anxiety. In C. D. Spielberger (Ed.), *Anxiety and behavior* (pp. 3-20). New York: Academic Press, 1966.

Spielberger, C. D., Gorsuch, R.L., & Lushene. R.E. (1970). *Manual for the State-Trait Anxiety Inventory*. Palo Alto, CA: Consulting Psychologists Press.

Spielberger, C.D. (1971). Trait-state anxiety and motor behavior. *Journal of Motor Behavior, 3*, 265-279.

Spielberger, C. D. (1972) Current trends in theory and research on anxiety. In C. D. Spielberger (Ed.) *Anxiety: Current trends in theory and research* (Vol. 1 pp. 3-19). New York: Academic Press.

Spielberger, C. D. (1972). Anxiety as an emotional state. In C. D. Spielberger (Ed.), *Anxiety: Current trends in theory and research* (Vol. 1 pp. 23-29). New York: Academic Press.

Spielberger, C. D. (1980). *Test anxiety inventory.* Palo Alto: Consulting Psychologists Press.

Spielberger, C. D. (1989). Stress and anxiety in sports. In D. Hackfort, & C. D. Spielberger, (Ed.), *Anxiety in sports: An international perspective* (pp. 3-13). New York: Hemisphere.

Stanislavski, C. (2003). *An actor prepares.* New York: Routledge.

Strelau, J., & Zawadzki, B. (1997). Temperament and personality: Eysenck's three superfactors as related to temperamental dimensions. In H. Nyborg (Ed.), *The scientific study of human nature: Tribute to Hans J. Eysenck at eighty* (pp. 68-91). New York: Pergamon.

Steptoe, A., Malik, F., & Pay, C.; Pearson, P., Price, C., Win, Z. (1995). The impact of stage fright on student actors. *The British Journal of Psychology, 86*, 27-39.

Strelau, J. and Zawadzki, B., (1997). Temperament and personality: Eysenck's three superfactors as related to temperamental dimensions. In: H. Nyborg, (Ed.) *The scientific study of human nature: Tribute to Hans J. Eysenck at eighty. (*pp. 68–91) Amsterdam: Elsevier.

Strong, C. M., Nowakowska, C., Santosa, C. M., Wang, P. W., Kraemer, H. C., & Ketter, T. A. (2005). Temperament-creativity relationships in mood disorder patients, healthy controls and highly creative individuals. *Journal of Affective Disorders, 100*, 41-48.

Stroud, M. W, Thorn, B. E., Jensen, M. P., et al. (2000). The relation between pain beliefs, negative thoughts, and psychosocial functioning in chronic pain patients. *Pain, 84*, 347-352.

Strube, M. J. (2005). What did Triplett really find? A contemporary analysis of the first experiment in social psychology. *The American Journal of Psychology, 118*(2) 271-286

Sussman, H. J. & Zahler, R. (1978a). Catastrophe theory as applied to the social and biological sciences. *Synthèse, 37*(2), 117-216.

Sussman, H. J. & Zahler, R. (1978b). A critique of applied catastrophe theory in applied behavioral sciences. *Behavioral Science 23*, 383-389.

Taylor, J. A. (1953). A personality scale of manifest anxiety. *Journal of Abnormal and Social Psychology, 48*, 285-290.

Taylor, J. A. (1956a). Drive theory and manifest anxiety. *Psychological Bulletin, 53,* 303-320.

Tellegen, A. (1985). Structures of mood and personality and their relevance to assessing anxiety with an emphasis on self-report. In A. H. Tuma & J. D. Maser (Eds.), *Anxiety and the anxiety disorders* (pp. 681-706). Hillsdale, NJ: Erlbaum.

Tellegen, A., Lykken, D. T., Bouchard, T. J., Wilcox, K., Segal, N., & Rich, S. (1988). Personality similarity in twins reared apart and together. *Journal of Personality and Social Psychology, 54*, 1031-1039.

Thayer, R. E. (1978). Toward a psychological theory of multidimensional activation (arousal). *Behavioral Science, 2*(1), 1573-6644. DOI: 10.1007/BF00992729

Thibaut, J. W., & Kelley, H. H. (1959) *The social psychology of groups*. New York: Wiley.

Thom, R. (1975). *Structural stability and morphogenesis.* Reading, MA: W.A. Benjamin. A. Wilson.

Thurstone, L. L. (1934). The vectors of the mind. *Psychological Review, 41*, 1-32.

Tolman, C. W. (1967). The feeding behaviour of domestic chicks a function of pecking by a surrogate companion. *Behaviour, 29*, 57-62.

Tolman, C. W. (1968). The varieties of social stimulation in the feeding behaviour of domestic chicks. *Behaviour, 30*, 275-286.

Travis, L. E. (1928). The Influence of the Group upon the Stutterer's Speed in Free Association. *Journal of Abnormal Social Psychology*, 23, 45-51.

Triplett, N. (1898). The dynamogenic factors in pacemaking and competition.*The American Journal of Psychology, 9*(4), 507-533.

Van Bockstaele, E. J., Menko, A. S., & Drolet, G. (2001). Neuroadaptations in brainstem noradrenergic nuclei following chronic morphine exposure. *Molecular Neurobiology 23*, 155-171.

Vygotsky, L. S. (1987). Thinking and speech. In R. W. Reiber and A. S. Carton (Eds.), (Trans., N. Minick), *The collected works of L. S. Vygotsky. Vol. 1: Problems of General Psychology.* New York, NY: Plenum.

Wahba, J. S., & McCroskey, J. C. (2005). Temperament and brain systems as predictors of assertive communication traits. *Communication Research Reports, 22*(2), 157-164.

Weinberg, R. S., & Gould, D. (1999). *Foundations of sport and exercise psychology* (2nd ed.). Champaign, IL: Human Kinetics.

Weiss, R. F., & Miller, F. G. (1971). The drive theory of social facilitation. *Psychological Review, 78,* 44-57.

Wesner, R. B., Noyes, R. Jr., & Davis, T. L. (1990). The occurrence of performance anxiety among musicians. *Journal of Affective Dis-*

cord, 18(2), 177-185.

Weston, S. B., & English, H. B. (1926). The influence of the group on psychological test scores. *The American Journal of Psychology, 37*, 600-601.

Wickham, G. (1985). *A history of theatre.* London: Cambridge University Press.

Wiggins, M.S., & Brustad, R.J. (1996). Perception of anxiety and expectations of performance. *Perceptual and Motor Skills, 83*(3 Part1), 1071-1047.

Wiggins, J. S., & Trapnell, P. D. (1997). Personality structure: The return of the Big Five. In R. Hogan, J. Johnson, & S. Briggs (Eds.), *Handbook of personality psychology* (pp.737-765). San Diego: Academic Press.

Williams, K., Harkins, S. & Latane, B. (1981). Identifiability as a deterrent to social loafing: two sheering experiments. *Journal of Personality and Social Psychology, 40*, 303-311.

Wilson, G. D. (2002) *Psychology for Performing Artists* (2nd Edition). London: Whurr.

Wine, J. (1971). Test anxiety and direction of attention. *Psychological Bulletin, 76*(2), 92-104.

Wine, J.D. (1980). Cognitive-attentional theory of test anxiety. In I. G. Sarason (Ed.), *Test anxiety: Theory, research, and applications* (pp. 349-385). Hillsdale, NJ: Erlbaum.

Wirtz, P. & Wawra, M. (1986). Vigilance and group size in Homo sapiens. *Ethology 71*,283-286.

Woodman, T., & Hardy, L. (2001). Stress and anxiety. In R.N. Singer, H.A. Hausenblas, & C.M. Janelle (Eds.), *Handbook of Sport Psychology.* pp. 290–318. New York: Wiley.

Woodman, T., & Hardy, L. (2003). The relative impact of cognitive anxiety and self-confidence upon sport performance: A meta-analysis. *Journal of Sports Sciences, 21*, 443-457.

Woodman, T., Davis, P. A., Hardy, L., Callow, N. Glasscock, I., & Yuill-Proctor, J. (2009). Emotions and sport performance: *An exploration of happiness, hope, and anger. Journal of Sport & Exercise Psychology, 31*(2), 169-188.

Yerkes, R. M. & Dodson, J. D. (1908). The Relation of Strength of Stimulus to Rapidity of Habit Formation. *Journal of Comparative and Neurological Psychology, 18*, 459-482.

Yokoo, H., Tanaka, M., Yoshida, M., Tsuda, A., Tanaka, T., and Mizoguchi, K. (1990). Direct evidence of conditioned fear-elicited enhancement or noradrenaline release in the rat hypothalamus assessed by intracranial microdialysis. *Brain Research, 536*, 305-308.

Yoshie, M., Shigemasu, K., Kudo, K., and Ohtsuki, T. (2009). Effects of state anxiety on music performance: Relationship between the Revised Competitive State Anxiety Inventory-2 subscales and piano performance. *Musicae Scientiae, 13*(1), 55-84.

Zajonc, R. B. (1965). Social facilitation. *Science, 149*, 269-274.

Zajonc, R. B., & Sales, S. M. (1966). Social facilitation of dominant and subordinate responses. *Journal of Experimental Social Psychology, 2*(2), 160-168.

Zajonc, R.B. (1968). Attitudinal Effects of Mere Exposure. *Journal of Personality and Social Psychology, 9*, 1-27.

Zajonc, R. B. (1980). Compresence. In P. B. Paulus (Ed.), *Psychology of group influence* (pp. 35-60). Hillsdale, NJ: Erlbaum.

Zajonc, R. B., Heingartner, A., Herman, E. M. (1969). Social enhancement and impairment of performance in the cockroach. *Journal of Personality and Social Psychology, 13*(2), 83-92.

Zillmann, D., & Bryant, J. (1994). Entertainment as Media Effect. *Media Effects: Advances in Theory and Research* (pp. 437-462) (Jennings Bryant and Dolf Zillmann, Eds). Hillsdale, NJ: Erlbaum

Zimbardo, P. G. (1977) *Shyness: What it is. What to do about it.* Reading, MA: Addison-Wesley.

ABOUT THE AUTHOR

Gordon Goodman is an American media psychologist and researcher in the field of performance anxiety. He began as a professional performer at age 16 and went on to perform as a baritone soloist with symphonies all over the world. He has been embedded in the field of creative and performing arts for decades, with experience in almost every performing arts venue.

A professional actor, he has had leading roles in dozens of musicals and plays, television performances, and over 25 television commercials. Dr. Goodman has developed or participated in the development of many large corporate events. He's authored many screenplays, stage plays, and full-length musicals (as composer and lyricist) as well as a number of books. He art directed and co-produced the *Puffy the Pillow Show* pilot for TV, and worked for a number of years with legendary producer, Chris Bearde, developing new television projects. His photography, charcoal portraits, paintings, illustrations, and sculptures are in private collections across the country. He owns the U.S. trademark for HypnoCast Educational Products. He is a certified hypnotherapist through the UCLA Medical School, two masters degrees, and a Ph.D. in psychology.

Gordon Goodman's Other Books Include:
The Knights of Royal Pond
Opera Goats
The Fish Who Had Fingers
Emma and the Gobbletygoos
The Castle of Mud
The Antelope and the Kangaroo

Other Works
The Hunchback of Notre Dame
Miss Palm Springs
Full Moon
Topless
Barrelman
Secret Santa
www.Gordon Goodman.com.

Stage Fright: Who Needs it?

www.ingramcontent.com/pod-product-compliance
Lightning Source LLC
Chambersburg PA
CBHW072013090426
42740CB00011B/2177